COOK'S COLLECTION

FAMILY FAVOURITES

*Fuss-free and tasty recipe ideas
for the modern cook*

CONTENTS

INTRODUCTION

✕

Everyone has favourite recipes. They're the ones you loved eating as a child or enjoyed when cooked by friends and wanted to repeat at home. Sometimes you're intrigued by recipes that you've seen in a magazine or on-line or even those handy little recipe cards at the supermarket checkout. Once you've cooked a new recipe for the family and it's been unanimously voted a hit, it tends to get added to your repertoire. Wherever recipes come from, it's the tried and tested ones that you cook most often – clean plates guaranteed!

Sometimes, though, making a few new additions to your menus is a good idea. It makes meals less predictable and boring and is a great way to encourage everyone to try new foods and flavours. *Family Favourites* is an easy-to-follow book packed full of recipes for modern cooks who want to prepare both everyday favourites and healthy meals that everyone will enjoy. Included are time-honoured classics such as comforting Chicken Noodle Soup (see page 84) and the perfect Double Macaroni Cheese (see page 61). But why not try

something a little different, such as the delicious Salmon Quinoa Burgers (see page 104), and serve them with a tangy Fresh Caribbean Salsa (see page 50)?

The advantage of making meals from scratch is that you know exactly what ingredients have gone into the recipe and you can be sure they're the freshest possible. Also, you control the seasonings and spices – great if you have fussy eaters to feed or children who are just starting to experience grown-up food. You'll also be assured you're giving your family the best possible wholesome and nourishing meals they'll all enjoy.

All this doesn't mean spending hours in the kitchen. At the end of a busy day it may be tempting to open a packet, take a ready meal from the freezer or order a takeaway. But you know in your heart of hearts that these are full of sugar and salt, which we don't need to overload our diet with. They're often quite pricey too. Why not get the family to help you plan meals for the week to fit in with everyone's timetable? You'll be able to see when you need quick-to-prepare meals that can be served straight away and when you have more time for slow-cooked dishes and experimenting with new recipes. If time allows, why not make double? You'll have a ready-made dish in the freezer to fall back on when time is at a premium. Make sure you label clearly, so you'll know how long to reheat for, and remember to take it out in plenty of time to thaw in the fridge.

Keep a rolling shopping list where everyone can see and add to it, so you'll be prepared when you head out to the supermarket or order a delivery on-line. It's a good idea to keep a stocked store cupboard with items such as tins of chopped tomatoes, beans, pastes and pesto, dried herbs and spices. A selection of pasta shapes, rice and any of the many available grains will always be useful for quick meals. There's a huge range of convenience foods out there that make a great addition to fresh ingredients. Make your fridge and freezer work for you by keeping them filled with the items you use the most so you're never caught without the means to produce a healthy, tasty meal that you can be proud of.

Take the opportunity to introduce a vegetarian meal once or twice a week. It's good to take a break from meat, and recipes such as Roasted Frittata Slices (see page 94) and Lentil & Mushroom Pie (see page 121) will soon become family favourites once you discover how versatile vegetables and pulses can be.

Fish is also a healthy addition to the diet. Why not turn Friday night into Fish Night for a healthy alternative to a take-away? You could try Fish & Potato Stew (see page 132) or Tuna & Broccoli Pasta Bake (see page 128). Both are quick and easy to prepare and will get rave reviews from the family.

Children are becoming more food aware these days and you may be surprised at their knowledge of recipes and ingredients. They enjoy being involved in simple preparation and supervised cooking, so, when the time is right, give them tasks that will help them feel that they're contributing to the family meal.

Save time with some advance preparation. Meat, poultry and fish can be cut up the night before or next morning and refrigerated, well covered. If the recipe calls for a marinade, make that too and add to the prepared food or store in a screw-top jar for a last-minute flavouring. Most vegetables can be peeled and cut up, packed in polythene zipped bags and put in the fridge. Chop onions, crush garlic and grate cheese in advance and keep a supply of soft breadcrumbs in the freezer for toppings.

The *Family Favourites* recipes aren't just for main meal dishes. We all know the benefits of breakfast, and having a few healthy options on hand will help ring the changes. For mornings when getting everyone out of the house on time is a challenge, wholesome bowls of Apple & Spice Oats (see page 12) will do just the trick. But on those slower, more leisurely weekends and holidays why not try Spinach & Nutmeg Baked Eggs (see page 34) and turn breakfast into brunch?

And who can forget desserts and the occasional treats? *Family Favourites* includes recipes for delicious pies, puddings, cookies and cakes that all the family will love. Mid-week meals don't always allow time for a home-made dessert, but when there's time, who can resist?

If you add the recipes in this book to your own tried and tested family favourites, you'll be able to enjoy preparing a huge range of delicious recipes for your loved ones.

CHAPTER ONE

BREAKFAST

CREAMY PORRIDGE
WITH BLACKBERRIES

SERVES: *2* | **PREP:** *5 mins* | **COOK:** *8 mins*

INGREDIENTS

100 g/3½ oz large rolled oats
small pinch of sea salt
600 ml/1 pint water
3½ tbsp double cream
1 tbsp demerara sugar
1 tbsp pumpkin seeds
6 large blackberries, quartered

1. Put the oats and salt in a medium-sized saucepan and pour over the water.

2. Bring to the boil, then reduce the heat to medium–low and simmer, stirring regularly, for 5–6 minutes, or until the oats are thick but have a dense pouring consistency.

3. Stir in the cream and sugar. Divide the porridge between two bowls, top with the pumpkin seeds and blackberry quarters and serve immediately.

PEAR, BANANA & APPLE
BREAKFAST BOWL

INGREDIENTS

2 ripe dessert pears

2 green-skinned apples, such as
  Granny Smith

1 large banana, peeled and
  chopped

75 ml/2½ fl oz apple juice

juice of ½ lemon

2 tbsp sultanas

2 tbsp raw cashew nuts

1 tbsp sunflower seeds

1 tbsp raw sugar

½ tsp ground cinnamon

1 tbsp goldenberries

1 tbsp cranberries

1. Core and chop one pear and one apple. Place them in a serving bowl with half the banana and pour over half the apple juice and half the lemon juice. Stir well to combine.

2. Core, peel and roughly chop the remaining pear and apple. Add them to a blender with the rest of the banana.

3. Add the remaining apple juice and lemon juice to the blender with the sultanas and nuts. Blend until you have a finely chopped mixture.

4. Stir the blended mixture into the chopped fruit, along with the sunflower seeds, sugar and cinnamon. Scatter over the goldenberries and cranberries. Chill in the fridge if you have time, or serve immediately.

APPLE &
SPICE OATS

INGREDIENTS

2 sprays of vegetable oil cooking
* spray*
2 large eggs
150 ml/5 fl oz skimmed milk
50 g/1¾ oz soft light brown sugar
115 g/4 oz apple sauce
1 tsp baking powder
½ tsp salt
½ tsp ground cinnamon
225 g/8 oz porridge oats
2 large red-skinned apples, cored
* and diced*
70 g/2½ oz dried fruit (raisins,
* apricots, cranberries, cherries or*
* a combination)*
1 tbsp unsalted butter, melted

1. Preheat the oven to 190°C/375°F/Gas Mark 5. Coat a shallow, wide ovenproof dish with cooking spray.

2. Beat the eggs and milk together in a bowl. Add the sugar, apple sauce, baking powder, salt and cinnamon and stir until thoroughly mixed. Stir in the oats, apples and dried fruit and mix well.

3. Spoon the mixture into the prepared dish, dot with butter, and bake in the preheated oven for 25 minutes, or until hot and bubbling.

THREE-GRAIN PORRIDGE
WITH RAISINS

SERVES: *4* | **PREP:** *10 mins* | **COOK:** *45 mins*

INGREDIENTS

40 g/1½ oz porridge oats

40 g/1½ oz quinoa flakes

40 g/1½ oz millet, rinsed

25 g/1 oz butter

900 ml/1½ pints water

pinch of salt

½ tsp ground cinnamon

¼ tsp vanilla extract

pinch of freshly grated nutmeg

90 g/3¼ oz raisins

*125 ml/4 fl oz milk or cream, to
serve*

4 tsp soft light brown sugar, to serve

1. Put the oats, quinoa flakes, millet and butter into a heavy-based non-stick saucepan. Place over a medium heat and stir for a few minutes until the butter has melted and the grains smell toasted.

2. Pour in the water, then add the salt, cinnamon, vanilla extract, nutmeg and raisins.

3. Bring to the boil, stirring constantly, over a low–medium heat. Reduce the heat and simmer gently for about 35 minutes, stirring frequently to prevent sticking, until the grains are tender but the millet still has some texture.

4. Divide the porridge between four bowls. Swirl in some milk, sprinkle with sugar to taste and serve immediately.

SUPER SEEDY
GRANOLA

SERVES: *6* | **PREP:** *20 mins* | **COOK:** *30–35 mins*

INGREDIENTS

150 g/5½ oz porridge oats
40 g/1½ oz pumpkin seeds
40 g/1½ oz sunflower seeds
40 g/1½ oz sesame seeds
1 tsp ground cinnamon
2 tbsp light muscovado sugar
2 tbsp olive oil
2 tbsp clear honey
juice of 1 small orange
40 g/1½ oz dried apple slices, diced
40 g/1½ oz dried blueberries
40 g/1½ oz dried cranberries

1. Preheat the oven to 160°C/325°F/Gas Mark 3. Add the oats, pumpkin seeds, sunflower seeds and sesame seeds to an 18 x 28-cm/7 x 11-inch roasting tin. Sprinkle with the cinnamon and sugar, and stir together.

2. Drizzle the oil, honey and orange juice over the top and mix together. Bake in the preheated oven for 30–35 minutes, stirring after 15 minutes and moving the mix in the corners to the centre as the edges will brown more quickly. Try to keep the granola in clumps. Return to the oven and stir every 5–10 minutes, until the granola is an even, golden brown.

3. Scatter the dried apple slices, blueberries and cranberries over the top and leave the granola to cool and harden. Spoon into a plastic container or preserving jar and store in the refrigerator for up to 4 days.

FRUIT & ALMOND MILK POWER BOWL

SERVES: *4* | **PREP:** *15 mins, plus soaking* | **COOK:** *No cooking*

INGREDIENTS

250 g/9 oz rolled oats

55 g/2 oz raisins

55 g/2 oz ready-to-eat dried apricots, chopped

55 g/2 oz flaked almonds

2 dessert apples, grated

600 ml/1 pint almond milk

4 tbsp Greek-style natural yogurt

55 g/2 oz raspberries

55 g/2 oz strawberries

55 g/2 oz blueberries

4 tbsp maple syrup

2 tbsp cacao nibs

1. Mix together the oats, raisins, apricots, almonds and apples in a large bowl.

2. Pour over the almond milk and mix well. Leave to soak overnight.

3. Divide between four bowls and top each portion with a dollop of yogurt, some raspberries, strawberries and blueberries, a drizzle of maple syrup and a sprinkling of cacao nibs. Serve immediately.

MINI ROASTED PEACH & RASPBERRY BLINIS

MAKES: *20* | **PREP:** *20 mins* | **COOK:** *25–30 mins*

INGREDIENTS

4 small peaches, halved, stoned and
  cut into chunks
1 tbsp maple syrup
2 tbsp water
150 g/5½ oz raspberries
150 g/5½ oz full-fat crème fraîche
1 tsp vanilla extract

BLINI BATTER

85 g/3 oz buckwheat flour
1 tsp baking powder
pinch of sea salt
1 egg, beaten
125 ml/4 fl oz milk
1 tbsp light olive oil, for frying

1. Preheat the oven to 190°C/375°F/Gas Mark 5. Place the peaches in a small roasting tin, drizzle over the maple syrup and water, then roast in the preheated oven for 10 minutes until soft and just beginning to brown around the edges. Remove from the oven, sprinkle the raspberries into the hot tin and set aside.

2. Mix the crème fraîche with the vanilla extract and set aside.

3. To make the blinis, put the flour, baking powder and salt into a bowl, and stir together. Add the egg, then gradually whisk in the milk until smooth.

4. Heat the oil in a large frying pan, then pour out the excess into a small bowl and set aside. Drop dessertspoons of the batter over the base of the pan, leaving a little space between each. Cook over a medium heat for 2–3 minutes until bubbles begin to show on the surface and the undersides are golden brown. Turn over with a palette knife and cook for a further 1–2 minutes.

5. Lift the blinis out of the pan with a palette knife and keep warm in a clean tea towel. Heat the reserved oil in the pan, pour out the excess, then continue cooking the blinis in batches until all the batter has been used up.

6. Layer the blinis on a large plate with the crème fraîche and warm fruit and serve immediately.

CARDAMOM WAFFLES
WITH BLACKBERRIES & FIGS

SERVES: *6* | **PREP:** *25 mins, plus resting* | **COOK:** *8–10 mins*

INGREDIENTS

5 large eggs, separated

pinch of salt

1 tsp ground cardamom

50 g/1¾ oz unsalted butter, melted and cooled

275 ml/9 fl oz milk

225 g/8 oz wholemeal plain flour

1 tbsp olive oil, for brushing

150 g/5½ oz Greek-style natural yogurt

6 ripe figs, quartered

200 g/7 oz blackberries

6 tbsp agave syrup, to serve

1. Place the egg yolks, salt and cardamom in a bowl and beat well with a wooden spoon. Stir in the butter. Slowly beat in the milk until fully incorporated. Gradually add the flour until a thick batter forms.

2. In a separate bowl, whisk the egg whites until they hold stiff peaks, then gently fold them into the batter. Leave the batter to rest for at least 1 hour, but preferably overnight.

3. Heat the waffle maker according to the manufacturers' instructions. Brush with a little oil and spoon some batter onto the waffle iron. Cook for 4–5 minutes, or until golden. Keep each waffle warm under foil in a low oven until you are ready to serve.

4. Serve the waffles topped with yogurt, fig quarters, blackberries and agave syrup.

STRAWBERRY & PASSION FRUIT YOGURTS

SERVES: *4* | **PREP:** *20–25 mins* | **COOK:** *2–3 mins*

INGREDIENTS

20 g/¾ oz desiccated coconut

200 g/7 oz strawberries, hulled

juice and finely grated zest of 1 lime

*350 g/12 oz Greek-style natural
  yogurt*

4 tsp clear honey

2 passion fruit, halved

*1 tbsp dried goji berries, roughly
  chopped*

1. Add the coconut to a dry frying pan and cook over a medium heat for 2–3 minutes, constantly shaking the pan, until light golden in colour. Remove from the heat and leave to cool.

2. Roughly mash the strawberries and mix with half the lime juice.

3. Add the lime zest, the remaining lime juice, the yogurt and honey to a bowl and stir together. Add three quarters of the cooled coconut to the yogurt, then scoop the seeds from the passion fruit over the top and lightly fold into the yogurt.

4. Layer alternate spoonfuls of strawberry and yogurt in four 200-ml/7-fl oz preserving jars, then sprinkle with the remaining coconut and the goji berries. Clip down the lids and chill until ready to serve. Eat within 24 hours.

RASPBERRY & APPLE SMOOTHIE

SERVES: *1* | **PREP:** *5–10 mins* | **COOK:** *No cooking*

INGREDIENTS

1 eating apple, peeled, cored and
*   chopped*
2 tbsp mineral water
55 g/2 oz raspberries
1 tsp clear honey (optional)
4 tbsp natural yogurt
ice cubes

1. Put the apple into a food processor or blender with the mineral water and blend for 1 minute.

2. Reserve 2–3 raspberries for decoration and add the remainder to the blender. Blend for 30 seconds, then add the honey, if using, and the yogurt. Blend for a further 1 minute.

3. Place a few ice cubes in a glass, pour over the smoothie, decorate with the reserved raspberries and serve immediately.

HOME-MADE CACAO
& HAZELNUT BUTTER

MAKES: *225 g/8 oz* | **PREP:** *15 mins, plus standing* | **COOK:** *3–4 mins*

INGREDIENTS

115 g/4 oz unblanched hazelnuts
25 g/1 oz raw cacao powder
70 g/2½ oz light muscovado sugar
125 ml/4 fl oz light olive oil
½ tsp natural vanilla extract
pinch of sea salt

1. Add the hazelnuts to a dry frying pan and cook over a medium heat for 3–4 minutes, constantly shaking the pan, until the nuts are an even golden brown in colour.

2. Wrap the nuts in a clean tea towel and rub to remove the skins.

3. Put the nuts into a blender and blend until finely ground. Add the cacao powder, sugar, oil, vanilla extract and salt and blend to a smooth paste.

4. Spoon into a small preserving jar and clip the lid in place. Leave to stand at room temperature for 4 hours until the sugar has dissolved completely. Stir again, then store in the refrigerator for up to 5 days.

FULL ENGLISH
BREAKFAST

SERVES: *1* | **PREP:** *10 mins* | **COOK:** *30–35 mins*

INGREDIENTS

2 good-quality pork sausages

2–3 smoked back bacon rashers

1 slice 2-day-old wholemeal bread

1 large tomato, halved

vegetable oil, for drizzling and
*   frying*

2–3 button mushrooms

1 egg

salt and pepper (optional)

1. Preheat the grill to high. Place the sausages under the hot grill and grill for about 15–20 minutes, turning frequently, until well browned. Keep warm.

2. Place the bacon rashers in a dry frying pan and fry for 2–4 minutes on each side. Remove from the pan, leaving all the excess bacon fat in the pan, and keep the bacon warm.

3. Reheat the fat over a medium heat and add the bread to the pan. Cook for 1–2 minutes on one side, then turn over and repeat. Remove from the pan and keep warm.

4. Place the tomato halves under the hot grill with the sausages. Drizzle with a little oil, season to taste with salt and pepper, if using, and grill for 3–4 minutes.

5. Add a little oil to a clean frying pan and fry the mushrooms. Remove from the pan and keep warm. Add the egg to the pan and fry, basting occasionally, for 1 minute, or until cooked to your liking.

6. Transfer the sausages, bacon, fried bread, tomatoes, mushrooms and egg to a warmed plate and serve immediately.

EGGY BREAD

SERVES: *2* | **PREP:** *10 mins* | **COOK:** *5 mins*

INGREDIENTS

1 large egg

4 tbsp milk or single cream

2 thick slices day-old white bread

25 g/1 oz butter

1. Break the egg into a shallow bowl and whisk well. Stir in the milk.

2. Dip the bread into the egg mixture and coat both sides well.

3. Melt half the butter in a frying pan over a medium heat and gently fry one piece of bread for about 1 minute on each side, or until golden brown and crispy. Take care not to let it burn. Remove from the pan and keep warm.

4. Melt the remaining butter and repeat with the remaining piece of bread. Serve immediately.

HOME-MADE
BAKED BEANS

SERVES: *4* | **PREP:** *10 mins* | **COOK:** *40 mins*

INGREDIENTS

200 g/7 oz tomatoes on the vine
1 tbsp olive oil
1 tbsp sesame seeds
1 tbsp pumpkin seeds
1 tbsp sunflower seeds
300 g/10½ oz roasted red peppers
2–3 tbsp vegetable stock
800 g/1 lb 12 oz canned haricot
    beans, drained
50 g/1¾ oz raisins
50 g/1¾ oz flaked almonds
15 g/½ oz fresh coriander
4 slices sourdough bread
4 eggs
salt and pepper (optional)

1. Preheat the oven to 200°C/400°F/Gas Mark 6.

2. Place the tomatoes in a roasting tin, sprinkle with the oil and salt and pepper, if using, and roast in the preheated oven for 20 minutes.

3. Meanwhile, add the sesame seeds, pumpkin seeds and sunflower seeds to a dry frying pan and fry for 2–3 minutes until starting to turn golden. Set aside.

4. Remove the tomatoes from the oven and blend in a blender with the red peppers and enough stock to loosen the sauce.

5. Pour the sauce into a saucepan, add the beans, bring to a simmer and simmer for 12–15 minutes.

6. Halfway through cooking stir in the raisins, half the flaked almonds and half the coriander.

7. Meanwhile, toast the bread on both sides. Bring a frying pan of water to a simmer. Break the eggs into a cup, one at a time, add to the pan and poach for 4–5 minutes. Remove the eggs from the pan and drain well.

8. Place the toast on four warmed plates and spoon over the beans. Top each serving with a poached egg and sprinkle over the remaining almonds and coriander, together with the toasted seeds. Serve immediately.

MUSHROOM & EGG CUPS WITH WHOLEMEAL TOAST

SERVES: *6* | **PREP:** *15 mins* | **COOK:** *20–25 mins*

INGREDIENTS

2 tbsp virgin olive oil

2 oak-smoked back bacon rashers,
  rind removed, diced

115 g/4 oz button mushrooms,
  sliced

3 eggs

125 ml/4 fl oz milk

40 g/1½ oz Cheddar cheese, grated

1 tbsp finely snipped fresh chives

200 g/7 oz cherry tomatoes on the
  vine

sea salt and pepper (optional)

6 slices wholemeal bread, to serve

1. Preheat the oven to 190°C/375°F/Gas Mark 5. Line the holes of a six-hole muffin tin with baking paper. Heat 1 tablespoon of the oil in a small frying pan over a medium–high heat. Add the bacon and fry for 2–3 minutes, or until just beginning to turn golden. Add the mushrooms and fry, stirring, for 2 minutes. Spoon the mixture into the holes in the prepared tin.

2. Crack the eggs into a jug, add the milk, cheese and chives and season to taste with salt and pepper, if using. Lightly beat with a fork until evenly mixed, then pour into the holes of the muffin tin. Stir so that the bacon and mushrooms are not all in the bases of the holes. Bake in the centre of the preheated oven for 15 minutes.

3. Put the tomatoes on a baking sheet, drizzle with the remaining oil and sprinkle with salt and pepper, if using. Place in the oven for the last 10 minutes of cooking time. Lightly toast the bread, then cut each slice in half.

4. Lift out the mushroom and egg cups, arrange on warmed plates with the toast and baked tomatoes and serve immediately.

SPINACH & NUTMEG BAKED EGGS

SERVES: *4* | **PREP:** *20 mins* | **COOK:** *20–30 mins*

INGREDIENTS

2 tbsp olive oil

4 shallots, finely chopped

3 garlic cloves, sliced

100 g/3½ oz baby spinach

8 eggs

½ tsp ground nutmeg

salt and pepper (optional)

1. Preheat the oven to 180°C/350°F/Gas Mark 4. Lightly brush the insides of four 200 ml/7 fl oz ramekins with half the oil.

2. Heat the remaining oil in a frying pan. Add the shallots and garlic and fry over a medium heat for 3–4 minutes, or until soft. Add the spinach and stir for 2–3 minutes, or until just wilted. Season to taste with salt and pepper, if using.

3. Spoon the spinach mixture into the bases of the prepared ramekins and crack two eggs into each. Sprinkle over the nutmeg and place the ramekins in a roasting tin. Fill the tin with boiling water until it reaches halfway up the ramekins – this creates a steamy environment for the eggs so there is no chance of them drying out.

4. Carefully transfer the tin to the preheated oven and bake the eggs for 15–20 minutes. Leave to cool slightly, then serve.

SWEET POTATO, SWEDE
& MUSHROOM HASH

SERVES: *4* | **PREP:** *15 mins* | **COOK:** *30 mins*

INGREDIENTS

3 tbsp olive oil

500 g/1 lb 2 oz sweet potatoes, diced

280 g/10 oz swedes, diced

1 onion, chopped

*175 g/6 oz sliced streaky bacon or
  lardons*

250 g/9 oz mushrooms, sliced

4 eggs

salt and pepper (optional)

*1 tbsp chopped fresh parsley,
  to garnish*

1. Heat the oil in a large frying pan with a tight-fitting lid over a high heat. Add the sweet potatoes and swedes, stir in the oil to coat and season to taste with salt and pepper, if using. Cook, stirring occasionally, for 10–15 minutes, or until just turning golden and soft.

2. Add the onion and bacon, stir well and cook for a further 5 minutes until the onion is soft and the bacon is cooked. Stir in the mushrooms, cover the pan and cook for a further 5 minutes.

3. Make four indentations in the mixture and carefully break an egg into each one. Cover the pan and cook for a further 3–4 minutes, or until the egg whites are firm but the yolks are still soft. Garnish with parsley and serve immediately.

KALE & POTATO CAKES
WITH FRIED EGGS

SERVES: *4* | **PREP:** *30 mins* | **COOK:** *35 mins*

INGREDIENTS

450 g/1 lb potatoes, unpeeled, cut into large chunks

100 g/3½ oz kale, thick stems removed

large knob of butter

4 spring onions, some green included, finely chopped,

2 tsp dill seeds

1 tsp finely grated lemon rind

5 tbsp vegetable oil

4 eggs

salt and pepper (optional)

1. Put the potatoes in a large saucepan of water with 1–2 teaspoons of salt, if using. Bring to the boil and cook for 15–20 minutes until tender but not disintegrating.

2. Meanwhile, bring a separate saucepan of water to the boil. Add the kale and blanch for 2 minutes. Drain and rinse under cold running water, squeezing out as much liquid as possible. Chop roughly.

3. Drain the potatoes, then return them to the pan for a few minutes to dry. Mash with the butter and salt and pepper to taste, if using.

4. Combine the potatoes, kale, spring onions, dill seeds and lemon rind in a large bowl, mixing well with a fork. Season to taste with salt and pepper, if using, and shape into four 1-cm/½-inch thick patties.

5. Heat 3 tablespoons of the oil in a large, non-stick frying pan over a medium heat. Add the patties and fry for 3–3½ minutes on each side, turning carefully, until golden. Set aside and keep warm.

6. Heat the remaining oil in the pan, break in the eggs and fry them until cooked to your liking. Place a fried egg on top of each patty and serve immediately.

THREE HERB
& RICOTTA OMELETTE

SERVES: *2* | **PREP:** *15 mins* | **COOK:** *8 mins*

INGREDIENTS

4 large eggs
2 tbsp finely snipped fresh chives
2 tbsp finely chopped fresh basil
2 tbsp finely chopped fresh parsley
100 g/3½ oz ricotta cheese,
  crumbled
2 tbsp olive oil
salt and pepper (optional)

1. Crack the eggs into a small bowl and lightly beat with a fork. Stir the chives, basil, parsley and cheese into the bowl and season to taste with salt and pepper, if using.

2. Heat the oil in a non-stick frying pan over a high heat until hot. Pour in the egg mixture and, using a spatula, draw the outside edges (which will cook more quickly) towards the gooey centre. Allow any liquid mixture to move into the gaps. Continue with this action for about 4–5 minutes. The omelette will continue to cook once the pan is removed from the heat.

3. Cut the omelette in half and divide between two plates. Serve immediately.

SPINACH &
PINE NUT FRITTATA

SERVES: *4* | **PREP:** *20 mins* | **COOK:** *20 mins*

INGREDIENTS

250 g/9 oz baby spinach

1 tbsp vegetable oil

25 g/1 oz butter

*1 large shallot, halved lengthways
   and finely sliced*

1 garlic clove, thinly sliced

40 g/1½ oz toasted pine nuts

¼ tsp dried red chilli flakes

8 eggs

*25 g/1 oz freshly grated Parmesan
   cheese*

salt and pepper (optional)

1. Wash the spinach thoroughly. Drain and put into a saucepan without any extra water. Cover and cook over a medium heat for 5 minutes, stirring occasionally, until just tender. Drain, squeezing out as much liquid as possible, then roughly chop.

2. Heat the oil and butter in a 24-cm/9½-inch non-stick frying pan over a medium heat. Add the shallot and fry for 3 minutes until translucent. Add the garlic and fry for a further 2 minutes. Stir in the spinach, pine nuts and chilli flakes. Season to taste with salt and pepper, if using.

3. Beat the eggs in a large jug with the cheese. Pour into the pan, stirring to distribute the spinach evenly. Cover and cook over a medium–low heat for 5–7 minutes until almost set. Meanwhile, preheat the grill to medium.

4. Place the pan under the preheated grill for 1–2 minutes to finish cooking the top of the frittata. Slice into wedges and serve.

CHAPTER TWO

SIDES & SNACKS

RED CABBAGE, ORANGE
& WALNUT COLESLAW

SERVES: *4* | **PREP:** *20 mins* | **COOK:** *No cooking*

INGREDIENTS

*100 g/3½ oz red cabbage, thinly
    shredded*
*100 g/3½ oz white cabbage, thinly
    shredded*
1 small red onion, thinly sliced
1 orange
40 g/1½ oz walnut pieces
handful of fresh coriander leaves

DRESSING

1½ tbsp walnut oil
2 tsp white wine vinegar
1 tsp Dijon mustard
1 tsp clear honey
½ tsp salt
pepper (optional)

1. Tip the red cabbage and white cabbage into a serving bowl.

2. Halve the onion slices and add to the bowl.

3. Using a sharp knife, cut a slice from the top and the bottom of the orange. Remove the peel and white pith by cutting downwards, following the shape of the fruit as closely as possible. Working over a small bowl to catch any juice, cut between the flesh and the membrane of each segment and ease out the flesh. Slice each segment in half. Squeeze the membrane over a small bowl to extract the juice. Add the orange pieces to the serving bowl.

4. To make the dressing, add the oil, vinegar, mustard, honey, salt, and pepper, if using, to the orange juice and whisk together.

5. Stir the dressing, walnut pieces and coriander leaves into the serving bowl. Serve immediately.

POTATO & CAULIFLOWER
SALAD

SERVES: 4 | **PREP:** 15–20 mins, plus standing | **COOK:** 35–40 mins

INGREDIENTS

300 g/10½ oz new potatoes
200 g/7 oz small cauliflower florets
4 tbsp extra virgin olive oil
4½ tsp red wine vinegar
200 g/7 oz fine French beans, cut
    into bite-sized pieces
4 spring onions, finely chopped
1 radish, thinly sliced
85 g/3 oz baby spinach leaves
2 tbsp toasted pine nuts
2 tbsp sultanas or raisins
salt and pepper (optional)
90 g/3¼ oz radicchio leaves,
    to serve
1 ciabatta loaf, thickly sliced,
    to serve

1. Add 1–2 teaspoons salt, if using, to two saucepans of water and bring to the boil. Add the potatoes to one pan, bring back to the boil and cook for 20–25 minutes until tender. Add the cauliflower florets to the other pan, bring back to the boil and cook for 5 minutes, or until tender-crisp.

2. Meanwhile, whisk together the oil, vinegar, and salt and pepper to taste, if using, in a serving bowl.

3. Use a large slotted spoon to remove the cauliflower florets from the pan, shaking off the excess water, and stir them into the dressing in the bowl.

4. Drop the beans into the cauliflower cooking water, bring back to the boil and cook for 5 minutes, or until tender-crisp. Drain well, then stir into the serving bowl.

5. Drain the potatoes and cool slightly under cold running water. Peel and cut into bite-sized pieces, then stir into the dressing together with the spring onions and radish. Make sure all the vegetables are coated with dressing, then set aside for at least 1 hour.

6. When ready to serve, line a platter with radicchio leaves. Stir the spinach into the serving bowl and add extra oil, vinegar and salt and pepper, if using. Stir in the pine nuts and raisins.

7. Spoon the salad onto the radicchio leaves, adding any dressing left in the bowl. Serve with the ciabatta bread to mop up the dressing.

CAESAR
SALAD

SERVES: *4* | **PREP:** *20–25 mins* | **COOK:** *5–10 mins*

INGREDIENTS

125 ml/4 fl oz olive oil

2 garlic cloves

5 slices white bread, crusts
    removed, cut into 1-cm/½-inch
    cubes

1 egg

3 Little Gem lettuces

2 tbsp lemon juice

8 canned anchovy fillets, drained
    and roughly chopped

salt and pepper (optional)

fresh Parmesan cheese shavings,
    to serve

1. Heat 4 tablespoons of the oil in a heavy-based frying pan. Add the garlic and bread and cook, stirring frequently, for 4–5 minutes until the bread is crisp and golden.

2. Remove the croûtons from the pan with a slotted spoon and drain on kitchen paper.

3. Meanwhile, bring a small saucepan of water to the boil. Add the egg and cook for 1 minute, then remove from the pan and set aside.

4. Arrange the lettuce leaves in a large bowl. In a separate bowl mix the remaining oil and the lemon juice with salt and pepper to taste, if using.

5. Crack the egg into the dressing and whisk to blend. Pour the dressing over the lettuce and toss well.

6. Add the chopped anchovies and croûtons, discarding the garlic, and toss the salad again.

7. Sprinkle with Parmesan cheese shavings and serve.

MIXED GREENS
& HERB SALAD

SERVES: *4* | **PREP:** *20 mins* | **COOK:** *No cooking*

INGREDIENTS

8 spring onions

55 g/2 oz watercress or rocket

55 g/2 oz frisée

*25 g/1 oz red mustard leaves, torn
    into bite-sized pieces*

*small handful of baby pak choi or
    baby kale leaves*

*small handful of fresh soft-leaf
    herbs, such as basil, mint,
    coriander and flat-leaf parsley*

large pinch of sea salt (optional)

3–4 tbsp hazelnut oil

*1 tbsp rice vinegar or white wine
    vinegar*

*55 g/2 oz toasted hazelnuts, roughly
    chopped*

1. Trim the spring onions, keeping some of the green parts. Slice lengthways into 2.5-cm/1-inch shreds.

2. Put the watercress, frisée, red mustard leaves, pak choi, herbs and spring onions into a large salad bowl. Sprinkle with the salt, if using, and gently toss with your hands to distribute it evenly.

3. Pour in enough of the oil to barely coat the leaves and gently toss. Add the vinegar and toss again.

4. Scatter the hazelnuts over the top and serve immediately.

FRESH CARIBBEAN SALSA

SERVES: *4* | **PREP:** *15 mins* | **COOK:** *No cooking*

INGREDIENTS

*1 large yellow pepper, deseeded and
cut into 1-cm/½-inch dice*
*½ cucumber, quartered, deseeded
and cut into 1-cm/½-inch dice*
2 slices fresh pineapple, chopped
2 spring onions, chopped
*2 fresh red chillies, deseeded and
finely chopped*
*handful of fresh coriander leaves,
to garnish*

DRESSING

juice of 1 lime
1 tsp jerk seasoning
1 tbsp extra virgin rapeseed oil

1. Put the yellow pepper, cucumber, pineapple, spring onions and chillies into a serving bowl.

2. To make the dressing, combine the lime juice, seasoning and oil in a small bowl.

3. Pour the dressing over the salad and stir thoroughly. Scatter the coriander leaves over the top and serve immediately.

STEAMED GREENS WITH
LEMON & CORIANDER

SERVES: *4* | **PREP:** *15 mins* | **COOK:** *10 mins*

INGREDIENTS

1 head of pointed spring cabbage,
tough outer leaves discarded
200 g/7 oz baby spinach
large knob of unsalted butter
finely grated rind of ½ lemon
4 tbsp chopped fresh coriander
sea salt and pepper (optional)

1. Cut the cabbage into quarters lengthways and cut out the tough stalk. Slice the quarters crossways into 2-cm/¾-inch ribbons. Place in a steamer and steam for 3 minutes until starting to soften.

2. Arrange the spinach on top of the cabbage, and steam for a further 3 minutes. Drain in a colander to remove any excess liquid.

3. Tip the cabbage and spinach into a warmed serving dish. Stir in the butter, lemon rind and coriander, mixing well.

4. Sprinkle with salt and pepper, if using, and serve immediately.

FRIED COURGETTES

SERVES: *4* | **PREP:** *15–20 mins, plus cooling* | **COOK:** *20–25 mins*

INGREDIENTS

2 tbsp olive oil, plus extra for
  drizzling
1 onion, finely chopped
2 large garlic cloves, finely chopped
400 g/14 oz courgettes, halved
  lengthways and thinly sliced
½ tsp dried oregano
150 ml/5 fl oz passata
salt and pepper (optional)
8 slices Italian bread, to serve

1. Heat the oil in a large frying pan over a medium heat. Add the onion, reduce the heat to low and fry, stirring, for 5–8 minutes until it is just starting to turn a pale golden colour. Stir in the garlic.

2. Add the courgettes and oregano and season to taste with salt and pepper, if using. Increase the heat to medium–high and fry, turning over the courgette slices occasionally, for 5–8 minutes until just starting to become tender.

3. Add the passata, bring to the boil and cook without stirring until the courgettes are tender but not mushy. Adjust the seasoning to taste, if using.

4. Transfer the courgettes to a warmed serving dish and drizzle with a little oil. Leave to cool, then serve with the bread.

CELERIAC &
NEW POTATO SMASH

SERVES: *4* | **PREP:** *15–20 mins* | **COOK:** *30 mins*

INGREDIENTS

1 small celeriac, peeled and cut into
   2-cm/¾-inch chunks
400 g/14 oz new potatoes, scrubbed
   and cut into 2-cm/¾-inch chunks
2 garlic cloves, crushed
1 tbsp olive oil
100 ml/3½ fl oz vegetable stock
½ tsp celery salt
2 tsp fresh thyme leaves
1 tbsp chopped fresh flat-leaf
   parsley
pepper (optional)

1. Put the celeriac into a large frying pan over a medium–high heat. Add the potatoes, garlic and oil and stir. Fry for 3–4 minutes, stirring occasionally, until the vegetables are lightly coloured.

2. Pour in the stock, add the celery salt, thyme and pepper, if using, and bring to a simmer. Cover and braise the vegetables for 20 minutes, adding a little water if they begin to look dry.

3. Using a potato masher, bash the vegetables in the pan – don't mash them, just break them down into smallish pieces. Sprinkle over the parsley, stir and serve immediately.

SLOW-COOKED PEPPERS
& ONIONS

SERVES: *4* | **PREP:** *15–20 mins* | **COOK:** *40 mins*

INGREDIENTS

3 tbsp olive oil

1 large onion, thinly sliced

3 mixed peppers, such as red,
* orange and yellow, deseeded and*
* cut into strips*

2 garlic cloves, finely chopped

400 g/14 oz canned chopped
* tomatoes*

2 tsp dried thyme

salt and pepper (optional)

1. Heat the oil in a large frying pan with a tight-fitting lid over a medium heat. Stir in the onion, cover, reduce the heat to low and simmer for 8–10 minutes until the onion is soft but not brown.

2. Stir in the mixed peppers and garlic and season to taste with salt and pepper, if using. Re-cover the pan and simmer for 5 minutes. Stir in the tomatoes and thyme and bring to the boil, stirring.

3. Reduce the heat to very low (use a heat diffuser if you have one), re-cover the pan and simmer for 20 minutes until the peppers are tender. If the sauce is too runny, uncover and boil until it reaches the desired consistency. Adjust the seasoning, if using.

4. Spoon into a serving dish and serve hot or at room temperature.

PERFECT
ROAST POTATOES

SERVES: *4* | **PREP:** *10-15 mins* | **COOK:** *1 hour–1 hour 10 mins*

INGREDIENTS

1.3 kg/3 lb large floury potatoes,
such as King Edward, Maris
Piper or Desirée, peeled and cut
into even-sized chunks
3 tbsp dripping, goose fat, duck fat
or olive oil
salt (optional)

1. Preheat the oven to 220°C/425°F/Gas Mark 7.

2. Add 1–2 teaspoons of salt, if using, to a large saucepan of water and bring to the boil, then add the potatoes and cook over a medium heat, covered, for 5–7 minutes. They will still be firm. Remove from the heat.

3. Meanwhile, add the fat to a roasting tin and place in the preheated oven.

4. Drain the potatoes well and return them to the pan. Cover with the lid and firmly shake the pan so that the surface of the potatoes is roughened. This will help give a much crisper texture.

5. Remove the tin from the oven and carefully tip the potatoes into the hot oil. Baste them to ensure they are all coated with the oil.

6. Roast at the top of the oven for 45–50 minutes until they are brown all over and thoroughly crisp. Turn and baste only once again during the process or the crunchy edges will be destroyed.

7. Carefully transfer the potatoes from the tin into a warmed serving dish. Sprinkle with a little salt, if using, and serve immediately.

DOUBLE CHEESE
MACARONI

SERVES: *4* | **PREP:** *20 mins* | **COOK:** *25–30 mins*

INGREDIENTS

225 g/8 oz dried macaroni
250 g/9 oz ricotta cheese
1½ tbsp wholegrain mustard
3 tbsp snipped fresh chives, plus
*   extra for sprinkling*
200 g/7 oz cherry tomatoes, halved
100 g/3½ oz sun-dried tomatoes in
*   oil, drained and chopped*
butter or oil, for greasing
100 g/3½ oz Cheddar cheese,
*   grated*
salt and pepper (optional)

1. Add 1–2 teaspoons of salt, if using, to a large saucepan of water and bring to the boil. Add the macaroni and cook for 10–12 minutes, or until tender but still firm to the bite. Drain.

2. Mix the ricotta cheese with the mustard, chives, and salt and pepper to taste, if using. Stir in the macaroni, cherry tomatoes and sun-dried tomatoes.

3. Grease a 1.7-litre/3-pint shallow ovenproof dish. Spoon in the macaroni mixture, spreading evenly.

4. Preheat the grill to high. Sprinkle the Cheddar cheese over the macaroni mixture and cook under the preheated grill for 4–5 minutes until golden and bubbling.

5. Serve the macaroni sprinkled with extra chives.

ROASTED VEGETABLES

SERVES: *4–6* | **PREP:** *30 mins* | **COOK:** *1 hour*

INGREDIENTS

*3 parsnips, cut into 5-cm/2-inch
    chunks*

4 baby turnips, cut into quarters

*3 carrots, cut into 5-cm/2-inch
    chunks*

*450 g/1 lb butternut squash, cut
    into 5-cm/2-inch chunks*

*450 g/1 lb sweet potatoes, cut into
    5-cm/2-inch chunks*

2 garlic cloves, finely chopped

*2 tbsp fresh rosemary, plus extra to
    garnish*

*2 tbsp fresh thyme, plus extra to
    garnish*

*2 tbsp fresh sage, plus extra to
    garnish*

3 tbsp olive oil

salt and pepper (optional)

1. Preheat the oven to 220°C/425°F/Gas Mark 7. Arrange all the vegetables in a single layer in a large roasting tin.

2. Scatter over the garlic, rosemary, thyme and sage. Pour over the oil and season to taste with salt and pepper, if using.

3. Toss all the ingredients together until they are well mixed and coated with the oil (if you have time you can leave them to marinate to allow the flavours to be absorbed).

4. Roast the vegetables at the top of the preheated oven for 1 hour until they are cooked and nicely browned. Turn them over halfway through the cooking time.

5. Serve with a good handful of fresh herbs scattered on top and a final sprinkling of salt and pepper to taste, if using.

BASIL & LEMON CAULIFLOWER RICE

SERVES: *4* | **PREP:** *20–25 mins* | **COOK:** *15–20 mins*

INGREDIENTS

70 g/2½ oz unskinned hazelnuts,
roughly chopped
1 head of cauliflower, about
500 g/1 lb 2 oz
1 tbsp olive oil
2 celery sticks, roughly chopped
3 garlic cloves, roughly chopped
25 g/1 oz fresh basil, roughly
chopped
juice and zest of 1 lemon
70 g/2½ oz watercress, chopped
salt and pepper (optional)

1. Add the hazelnuts to a large, dry frying pan. Toast over a medium heat until golden. Remove from the pan and set aside.

2. Remove the core from the cauliflower and divide up the florets. Place in a food processor and pulse until the cauliflower resembles rice grains. Place in a bowl and set aside.

3. Place the oil in a frying pan over a medium heat, add the celery and garlic and fry for about 5–6 minutes, or until soft.

4. Add the cauliflower rice to the pan and stir to combine. Cook, stirring occasionally, for 8–10 minutes. Remove from the heat and leave to cool for a few minutes before adding the basil, lemon zest, lemon juice, toasted hazelnuts and watercress. Season to taste with salt and pepper, if using, and serve immediately.

STUFFED
ROAST TOMATOES

SERVES: *4* | **PREP:** *15 mins* | **COOK:** *25–30 mins*

INGREDIENTS

1 tbsp olive oil
1 small red onion, finely chopped
1 garlic clove, finely chopped
8 large tomatoes
60 g/2¼ oz feta cheese, crumbled
25 g/1 oz pine nuts
6 tbsp finely chopped fresh flat-leaf
  parsley
sea salt and pepper (optional)

1. Preheat the oven to 180°C/350°F/Gas Mark 4. Heat the oil in a saucepan over a medium heat. Add the onion and garlic and cook for 5–10 minutes, or until the onion is translucent. Tip into a large bowl and leave to cool.

2. Meanwhile, using a small, sharp knife, cut a round with a diameter of 2.5 cm/1 inch from the stem of each tomato to make a 'lid'. Using a small spoon, scoop out the seeds and discard.

3. Mix the cheese, pine nuts and parsley into the onion and garlic mixture and season to taste with salt and pepper, if using. Stuff the tomatoes with this mixture, pressing down well with the back of a spoon.

4. Place a 'lid' on each tomato and transfer to a shallow baking dish. Roast in the preheated oven for 20 minutes, or until completely soft. Serve warm.

HOME-MADE HUMMUS

SERVES: *4* | **PREP:** *15–20 mins* | **COOK:** *No cooking*

INGREDIENTS

400 g/14 oz canned chickpeas,
*   drained and rinsed*
3 tbsp tahini
25 g/1 oz fresh basil, roughly
*   chopped, plus extra leaves to*
*   garnish*
pinch of paprika
2 garlic cloves
finely grated zest and juice of
*   1 lemon*
4–5 tbsp water
salt and pepper (optional)

1. Place the chickpeas, tahini, basil, paprika, garlic and lemon zest and juice in a food processor and process until coarse.

2. With the food processor still running, slowly add the water until a smooth, thick paste forms, adding a little more water if needed. Season to taste with salt and pepper, if using.

3. Garnish with basil leaves and serve immediately or place in a covered container and keep in the refrigerator. The hummus will keep in the refrigerator for up to 3 days.

CHEESY QUINOA CRACKERS WITH TOMATO SALSA

SERVES: *4* | **PREP:** *35 mins* | **COOK:** *12–15 mins*

INGREDIENTS

40 g/1½ oz golden linseeds, plus
extra for sprinkling
115 g/4 oz quinoa flour
½ tsp mustard powder
¼ tsp sea salt
pinch of cayenne pepper
55 g/2 oz butter, diced
55 g/2 oz mature Cheddar cheese,
finely grated
2 eggs, 1 beaten, 1 separated
1 tbsp sesame seeds

SALSA

2 tomatoes, cut into wedges
1 spring onion, sliced
2–3 fresh coriander sprigs
salt and pepper (optional)

1. Preheat the oven to 190°C/375°F/Gas Mark 5. Grind the linseeds in a spice mill to a coarse flour, then tip into a bowl and stir in the flour, mustard powder, sea salt and cayenne pepper.

2. Add the butter and rub it in with your fingertips until the mixture resembles fine crumbs. Stir in the cheese, then mix in the egg and egg yolk, and press together with your hands to make a rough dough.

3. Gently knead the dough, then place between two sheets of non-stick baking paper, roll out to a rectangle and trim to 25 x 20 cm/ 10 x 8 inches. Cut into 2.5 x 10-cm/1 x 4-inch crackers. Leave the crackers on the paper and separate them slightly, then slide a baking sheet under the paper.

4. Lightly beat the egg white, then brush over the crackers and sprinkle with the sesame seeds and some linseeds. Bake in the preheated oven for 12–15 minutes, until golden, then leave to cool on the paper.

5. Meanwhile, make the salsa by finely chopping the tomatoes, spring onion and coriander. Season to taste with salt and pepper, if using. Serve the salsa with the crackers.

MINI CHEESE
& POTATO FRITTATAS

MAKES: *12* | **PREP:** *17–20 mins* | **COOK:** *25–30 mins*

INGREDIENTS

100 g/3½ oz waxy potatoes,
* unpeeled and scrubbed*
1 tbsp olive oil or sunflower oil, for
* greasing*
4 eggs
125 ml/4 fl oz milk
2 chargrilled red peppers in oil,
* drained and finely chopped*
85 g/3 oz freshly grated Parmesan
* cheese or pecorino cheese*
2 tbsp finely snipped chives
salt and pepper (optional)

1. Add 1–2 teaspoons of salt, if using, to a saucepan of water and bring to the boil. Add the potatoes, bring back to the boil and cook for 12–15 minutes until tender. Drain well and cool under cold running water.

2. Meanwhile, preheat the oven to 190ºC/375ºF/Gas Mark 5. Generously grease a 12-hole muffin tin. When the potatoes are cool enough to handle, peel and finely chop them, then squeeze out the excess moisture.

3. Beat the eggs and milk together in a bowl. Stir in the potatoes, red peppers, two thirds of the cheese and all of the chives. Season to taste with salt and pepper, if using.

4. Divide the mixture equally between the holes in the prepared tin, filling each just under half full. Sprinkle the remaining cheese over the tops of the frittatas, taking care not to get it on the edges.

5. Place the tin in the preheated oven and bake for 25–30 minutes, until the frittatas are set and golden brown.

6. Remove the tin from the oven and run a round-bladed knife around each one, then tip them out. Transfer to a platter and either serve immediately or leave to cool to room temperature.

BLUEBERRY GRANOLA BARS

MAKES: *12* | **PREP:** *20 mins, plus cooling* | **COOK:** *25 mins*

INGREDIENTS

115 g/4 oz dried blueberries
225 g/8 oz rolled oats
40 g/1½ oz soft light brown sugar
50 g/1¾ oz pecan nuts, chopped
25 g/1 oz sunflower seeds
1 tbsp sesame seeds
¼ tsp ground cinnamon
115 g/4 oz golden syrup
115 g/4 oz butter, plus extra
*   for greasing*

1: Preheat the oven to 180°C/350°F/Gas Mark 4. Grease an 18 x 28-cm/7 x 11-inch baking tin.

2: Put the blueberries, oats, sugar, nuts, sunflower seeds, sesame seeds and cinnamon into a large bowl.

3: Put the golden syrup and butter into a saucepan over a low heat and heat until just melted. Stir in the dry ingredients until well coated in the butter mixture. Transfer the mixture to the prepared tin and smooth the surface.

4: Place in the preheated oven and bake for 20 minutes until golden. Remove from the oven and leave to cool for 5 minutes before marking into 12 bars.

5: Leave to cool completely in the tin, then cut through the markings to make 12 bars.

SUPERFOOD
CHOCOLATE BARK

SERVES: *6* | **PREP:** *20 mins, plus setting* | **COOK:** *5 mins*

INGREDIENTS

100 g/3½ oz plain chocolate, 70%
cocoa solids, broken into pieces
85 g/3 oz mixed Brazil nuts,
unblanched almonds and
pistachio nuts, roughly chopped
2 tbsp dried goji berries, roughly
chopped
2 tbsp dried cranberries, roughly
chopped
1 tbsp chia seeds

1. Place the chocolate in a heatproof bowl set over a saucepan of gently simmering water and heat until melted.

2. Line a large baking sheet with non-stick baking paper. Stir the chocolate, then pour it onto the paper and spread to a 20 x 30-cm/ 8 x 12-inch rectangle.

3. Sprinkle the nuts, goji berries, cranberries and chia seeds over the top, then leave to set in a cool place or the refrigerator.

4. To serve, lift the chocolate off the paper and break into rough-shaped shards. Store in a plastic container in the refrigerator for up to 3 days.

HOT CHOCOLATE
STICKS

MAKES: *10–15* | **PREP:** *5–10 mins* | **COOK:** *5–10 mins*

INGREDIENTS

*200 g/7 oz plain chocolate, milk
chocolate or white chocolate, or a
mixture, finely chopped*
2–4 tbsp instant coffee granules
2–4 tbsp desiccated coconut
2–4 tbsp toasted nuts
2–4 tbsp mini marshmallows
2–4 tbsp chocolate vermicelli
2–4 tbsp edible glitter
1.2 litres/2 pints milk, to serve

1. Put the chocolate into a heatproof bowl set over a saucepan of gently simmering water and heat until melted. If you are using different chocolates melt them in separate bowls.

2. Divide the chocolate between silicone moulds, a silicone ice tray or small paper cases. Leave to cool slightly until the chocolate begins to thicken, then push a small wooden spoon, lollipop stick or wooden coffee stirrer into each mould so it stands upright.

3. While the chocolate is still soft, scatter the sticks with: instant coffee granules, dessicated coconut, toasted nuts, mini marshmallows, chocolate vermicelli and edible glitter, then leave to set solid.

4. To serve, heat 1 mug of milk for each chocolate chunk stick. Remove any paper cases and stir a stick into each mug of milk until melted. Serve immediately.

ALMOND MILK
& COOKIE CUPS

MAKES: *6* | **PREP:** *25 mins, plus chilling* | **COOK:** *18–20 mins*

INGREDIENTS

6 tbsp coconut oil, at room
temperature, plus extra for oiling
55 g/2 oz light muscovado sugar
½ tsp natural vanilla extract
25 g/1 oz ground hazelnuts
25 g/1 oz ground golden linseeds
115 g/4 oz plain wholemeal flour
1 egg yolk
100 g/3½ oz plain chocolate, 70%
cocoa solids
150 ml/5 fl oz unsweetened almond
milk

1. Lightly oil six 90-ml/3-fl oz dariole moulds and line the base of each with a round of non-stick baking paper.

2. Beat together the oil, sugar and vanilla extract in a mixing bowl or food processor until light and creamy. Add the hazelnuts and linseeds, then add the flour and egg yolk and beat together. Finely chop 25 g/1 oz of the chocolate and mix it into the cookie crumbs. Using your hands, squeeze the dough into crumbly clumps.

3. Divide the mixture between the prepared moulds, then smooth it with the back of a teaspoon. Transfer to a baking tray and chill in the refrigerator for 20 minutes. Meanwhile, preheat the oven to 180°C/350°F/Gas Mark 4.

4. Place the tray in the preheated oven and bake for 13–15 minutes until golden brown, then reshape the inside of the cups with the back of a small teaspoon. Leave to cool for 30 minutes.

5. Loosen the edges of the cups with a small, round-bladed knife and remove from the tin. Return to the tray and chill in the refrigerator for at least 1 hour until firmly set.

6. Break the remaining chocolate into a heatproof bowl set over a saucepan of very gently simmering water and heat until melted. Add spoonfuls of melted chocolate to the cookie cups, tilting to cover the insides evenly with chocolate. Chill in the refrigerator for at least 30 minutes, then pour in the almond milk and serve on small saucers.

CHAPTER THREE

LUNCH

ROAST SQUASH SOUP
WITH CHEESE TOASTIES

SERVES: *4* | **PREP:** *20 mins* | **COOK:** *1 hour 5 mins–1 hour 15 mins*

INGREDIENTS

*1 kg/2 lb 4 oz butternut squash, cut
   into small chunks*

2 onions, cut into wedges

2 tbsp olive oil

2 garlic cloves, crushed

*3–4 fresh thyme sprigs, leaves
   removed*

1 litre/1¾ pints vegetable stock

150 ml/5 fl oz crème fraîche

salt and pepper (optional)

fresh chives, to garnish

CHEESE TOASTIES

1 baguette, thinly sliced diagonally

40 g/1½ oz Cheddar cheese, grated

1. Preheat the oven to 190°C/375°F/Gas Mark 5. Place the squash, onions, oil, garlic and thyme in a roasting tin. Toss together and spread out in a single layer. Roast in the preheated oven for 50 minutes–1 hour, stirring occasionally, until the vegetables are tender and caramelized in places.

2. Transfer the vegetables to a saucepan. Add half the stock and purée with a hand-held blender until smooth. Stir in the remaining stock and the crème fraîche. Season to taste with salt and pepper, if using, and heat through gently.

3. To make the toasties, preheat the grill to high. Toast the sliced baguette under the preheated grill for 1–2 minutes on each side until pale golden in colour. Sprinkle with the cheese and return to the grill for a further 30–40 seconds until melted and bubbling.

4. Ladle the soup into warmed bowls, sprinkle with chives and serve immediately with the cheese toasties on the side.

CHICKEN
NOODLE SOUP

SERVES: *4* | **PREP:** *15 mins* | **COOK:** *25–30 mins*

INGREDIENTS

1 tbsp groundnut oil
1 onion, finely chopped
2 celery sticks, finely chopped
1 large carrot, finely chopped
2 garlic cloves, crushed
*400 g/14 oz skinless, boneless
    chicken breasts, cut into bite-
    sized pieces*
*150 g/5½ oz fine French beans, cut
    into 3-cm/1¼-inch pieces*
1.2 litres/2 pints chicken stock
*150 g/5½ oz dried wholemeal egg
    noodles*
pepper (optional)
*small bunch of fresh coriander
    leaves, to garnish*

1. Heat the oil in a saucepan over a medium heat. Add the onion, celery and carrot and cook, stirring occasionally, for 8 minutes, until soft but not brown.

2. Add the garlic and cook for 1 minute. Add the chicken to the pan with the beans, stock and pepper, if using. Bring to the boil, then reduce the heat and simmer for 5 minutes.

3. Add the noodles to the pan, bring back to a simmer and cook for 5 minutes, or until the noodles are just tender. Garnish the soup with coriander leaves and serve immediately.

CAULIFLOWER SOUP

SERVES: *6* | **PREP:** *20 mins* | **COOK:** *45–50 mins*

INGREDIENTS

1 tbsp olive oil

25 g/1 oz butter

1 large onion, roughly chopped

2 leeks, sliced

1 large head of cauliflower

900 ml/1½ pints vegetable stock

salt and pepper (optional)

grated Cheddar cheese, to serve

extra virgin olive oil, to serve

1. Heat the oil and butter in a large saucepan, add the onion and leeks and fry for 10 minutes, stirring frequently, taking care not to allow the vegetables to colour.

2. Cut the cauliflower into florets and cut the stalk into small pieces. Add to the pan and sauté with the other vegetables for 2–3 minutes.

3. Add the stock and bring to the boil, cover and simmer over a medium heat for 20 minutes.

4. Pour the soup into a food processor or blender, process until smooth and return to the rinsed-out pan. Heat the soup through, season to taste with salt and pepper, if using, and serve in warmed soup bowls, topped with some grated cheese and a drizzle of oil.

TOMATO, LENTIL
& RED PEPPER SOUP

SERVES: 4 | **PREP:** 15 mins, plus cooling | **COOK:** 50 mins

INGREDIENTS

3 tbsp olive oil

2 onions, chopped

1 garlic clove, finely chopped

2 large red peppers, deseeded and
    chopped

500 g/1 lb 2 oz ripe tomatoes,
    chopped

100 g/3½ oz red split lentils

600 ml/1 pint vegetable stock, plus
    extra for thinning (optional)

1 tbsp red wine vinegar

pepper (optional)

2 spring onions, chopped, or 1 tbsp
    snipped fresh chives, to garnish

1. Heat the oil in a large saucepan over a medium–high heat, add the onions and cook, stirring, for 5 minutes, or until soft but not brown. Add the garlic and red peppers and cook, stirring, for 5 minutes, or until the red peppers are soft.

2. Add the tomatoes, lentils and stock and bring to a simmer. Reduce the heat to low, cover and simmer gently for 25 minutes, or until the lentils are tender. Stir in the vinegar and season to taste with pepper, if using.

3. Leave to cool slightly, then transfer the soup to a blender or food processor and blend for 1 minute, or until smooth. Return to the pan and reheat, stirring in a little hot water or stock if the soup seems a little too thick. Serve in warmed soup bowls, garnished with the spring onions.

GRILLED CHICKEN
& SLAW BOWL

SERVES: *4* | **PREP:** *25 mins* | **COOK:** *8–10 mins*

INGREDIENTS

4 x 150-g/5½-oz boneless, skinless
chicken breasts
1 tsp smoked paprika
salt and pepper (optional)
12 fresh rocket leaves, to garnish

COLESLAW

2 carrots, peeled and grated
1 fennel bulb, trimmed and thinly
sliced
1 beetroot, grated
150 g/5½ oz red cabbage, shredded
150 g/5½ oz white cabbage,
shredded
4 radishes, thinly sliced
1 red onion, peeled and thinly sliced
15 g/½ oz fresh mixed herbs,
such as parsley, dill, mint and
coriander, chopped
juice of 1 lemon
2 tbsp extra virgin olive oil
250 g/9 oz natural yogurt
1 tbsp wholegrain mustard

1. To make the coleslaw, put all the ingredients into a large bowl.
Toss together until well combined and set aside.

2. Preheat the grill to medium. Place the chicken breasts between
two sheets of greaseproof paper and flatten with a rolling pin or
mallet to a thickness of 1–2 cm/½–¾ inch.

3. Season the chicken with paprika, and salt and pepper, if using.
Grill for 4–5 minutes on each side until the chicken is tender and the
juices run clear when a skewer is inserted into the thickest part of
the meat.

4. Divide the coleslaw between four bowls, top with the chicken
slices and rocket leaves and serve immediately.

SALAD-PACKED OPEN SANDWICH

SERVES: *1* | **PREP:** *10 mins* | **COOK:** *2 mins*

INGREDIENTS

15 g/½ oz pine nuts

100 g/3½ oz quark

1 thick slice mixed grain bread

1 tomato, sliced

3-cm/1¼-inch piece cucumber,
* sliced*

½ small avocado, sliced

10 g/¼ oz wild rocket

2 fresh basil sprigs, leaves picked
* and torn*

1 tbsp aged balsamic vinegar

½ tsp pepper (optional)

2 tsp freshly grated Parmesan
* cheese*

1. Place a small frying pan over a high heat, add the pine nuts and toast until golden. Spread the quark on the bread.

2. Arrange the tomato, cucumber and avocado slices on top of the bread. Sprinkle over the rocket and basil.

3. Sprinkle over the pine nuts, vinegar and pepper, if using, and finish with the cheese. Cut into quarters and serve immediately.

STEAK SANDWICHES
WITH CARAMELIZED ONIONS

SERVES: *4* | **PREP:** *20 mins* | **COOK:** *50 mins, plus resting*

INGREDIENTS

2 sirloin steaks, each weighing
  about 225 g/8 oz
2 red onions, sliced into thick rings
3 tbsp olive oil, plus extra for
  brushing and drizzling
2 tsp sugar
2 tsp balsamic vinegar
8 slices sourdough bread
1 beef tomato, sliced
50 g/1¾ oz rocket
salt and pepper (optional)

1. Preheat the oven to 190°C/375°F/Gas Mark 5.

2. Lightly brush the steaks with oil, sprinkle with salt and pepper, if using, and set aside at room temperature.

3. Put the onion rings in a large bowl with the oil, sugar and salt and pepper to taste, if using. Toss well, separating the rings. Spread out in a roasting tin and roast in the preheated oven for 20–25 minutes, stirring every 10 minutes, until just beginning to brown. Sprinkle with the vinegar, stir and spread out again. Roast for a further 5–8 minutes until brown and sticky. Tip into a bowl and set aside.

4. Heat a ridged griddle pan over a medium–high heat. Add the steaks and fry for 3–3½ minutes on each side. Transfer to a board and leave to rest for 5 minutes. Preheat the grill to medium.

5. Place the bread under the preheated grill and toast on both sides. Arrange the tomato slices and rocket on four of the toast slices. Drizzle with a little oil and sprinkle with salt and pepper, if using.

6. Carve each steak diagonally into 2-cm/¾-inch slices. Arrange on top of the rocket, then add a few caramelized onion rings (any leftover onions can be stored in an airtight container in the refrigerator for up to 1 month). Top with the remaining toast slices and serve immediately.

ROASTED
FRITTATA SLICES

SERVES: *8* | **PREP:** *15-20 mins* | **COOK:** *1 hour 10 mins, plus cooling*

INGREDIENTS

1 head of Romanesco cauliflower,
  outer leaves removed, about
  600 g/1 lb 5 oz total weight
125 ml/4 fl oz olive oil
1 onion, chopped
1 tsp fresh thyme leaves
8 eggs
5 tbsp chopped fresh flat-leaf
  parsley
115 g/4 oz plain flour
1½ tsp baking powder
125 g/4½ oz mature Cheddar
  cheese, coarsely grated
1 large salad onion, some green
  included, thinly sliced diagonally
3 small ripe tomatoes, sliced
4 tbsp coarsely grated Parmesan
  cheese
salt and pepper (optional)

1. Preheat the oven to 220°C/425°F/Gas Mark 7. Line a 26 x 22-cm/10½ x 8½-inch roasting tin with baking paper.

2. Slice the cauliflower lengthways into quarters, discarding the tough central stem. Slice into small florets. Spread out in a roasting tin and sprinkle with 3 tablespoons of the oil, ¾ teaspoon of salt and ½ teaspoon of pepper, if using.

3. Cover tightly with foil and roast in the preheated oven for 15 minutes. Remove the foil, stir and roast for a further 10 minutes, or until golden at the edges. Remove from the oven and leave to cool. Reduce the oven temperature to 180°C/350°F/Gas Mark 4.

4. Meanwhile, heat 2 tablespoons of the remaining oil in a frying pan. Add the onion and thyme and fry over a medium heat for about 10 minutes until soft, then remove from the heat and leave to cool.

5. In a large bowl, beat the eggs with the remaining oil, the onion mixture and the parsley. Whisk in the flour, baking powder and salt and pepper to taste, if using. Stir in the Cheddar cheese and the cauliflower.

6. Pour the mixture into the prepared tin. Scatter the salad onion and tomatoes over the top, then sprinkle with the Parmesan cheese. Bake for 30 minutes, or until a knife inserted into the centre of the frittata comes out clean.

7. Remove from the oven and leave to cool in the tin for 15 minutes. Cut into eight slices and serve warm or at room temperature.

PULLED PORK
WRAPS

SERVES: *4* | **PREP:** *20 mins* | **COOK:** *3 hours 50 mins, plus resting*

INGREDIENTS

1 small pork shoulder joint, skin
removed, about 1 kg/2 lb 4 oz
total weight
1 tsp salt
2 tsp sweet paprika
2 tsp soft light brown sugar
1 tsp Dijon mustard
100 ml/3½ fl oz reduced-salt
chicken stock

TO SERVE

8 crisp lettuce leaves
6 spring onions, chopped
¼ cucumber, chopped
20 g/¾ oz fresh coriander leaves
1 mild red chilli
3 tbsp chilli dipping sauce
juice of ½ lime
4 multigrain tortillas

1. Preheat the oven to 220°C/425°F/Gas Mark 7. Line a roasting tin with a sheet of foil large enough to cover the pork. Place the pork in the tin, rub ½ teaspoon of the salt and 1 teaspoon of the paprika into the skin and cook, uncovered, in the preheated oven for 30 minutes.

2. Reduce the oven temperature to 150°C/300°F/Gas Mark 2. Rub the remaining salt and paprika into the pork with the sugar and mustard. Pour in the stock and loosely cover with the foil. Cook for a further 3 hours, or until the pork is soft and a piece comes away from the joint with ease when pulled with a fork.

3. Increase the oven temperature to 220°C/425°F/Gas Mark 7 and cook the pork for a further 20 minutes until crisp on the outside. Remove from the oven and leave to rest, covered, for 30 minutes.

4. Pull the pork into pieces with two forks. Pour any cooking juices over the pulled pork and stir to combine. Use 400 g/14 oz of the pork to make the wraps.

5. Divide the pork, lettuce, spring onions, cucumber, coriander, chilli, chilli sauce and lime juice between the tortillas. Serve immediately.

ROASTED VEGETABLE & FETA CHEESE WRAPS

SERVES: *4* | **PREP:** *20–25 mins* | **COOK:** *20–25 mins*

INGREDIENTS

1 red onion, cut into eighths

1 red pepper, deseeded and cut into eighths

1 small aubergine, cut into eighths

1 courgette, cut into eighths

4 tbsp extra virgin olive oil

1 garlic clove, crushed

100 g/3½ oz feta cheese, crumbled

small bunch fresh mint, shredded

4 sun-dried tomato wraps

salt and pepper (optional)

1. Preheat the oven to 220°C/425°F/Gas Mark 7. Mix together the vegetables, oil and garlic, season to taste with salt and pepper, if using, and arrange in a single layer on a non-stick baking tray. Roast in the preheated oven for 15–20 minutes, or until soft and golden.

2. Remove from the oven and leave to cool, then add the cheese and mint and mix to combine.

3. Preheat a non-stick frying pan or griddle pan until almost smoking, then add the wraps one at a time and cook for 10 seconds on each side.

4. Divide the vegetable and cheese mixture between the wraps, placing some along the middle of each wrap.

5. Roll up the wraps, cut them in half and serve immediately.

CHICKEN
FAJITAS

SERVES: *4* | **PREP:** *25 mins, plus marinating* | **COOK:** *10–15 mins*

INGREDIENTS

3 tbsp olive oil, plus extra for
*   drizzling*
3 tbsp maple syrup or clear honey
1 tbsp red wine vinegar
2 garlic cloves, crushed
2 tsp dried oregano
1–2 tsp dried chilli flakes
4 skinless, boneless chicken breasts
2 red peppers, deseeded and cut into
*   2.5-cm/1-inch strips*
salt and pepper (optional)
4 warmed flour tortillas, to serve
shredded lettuce, to serve

1. Place the oil, maple syrup, vinegar, garlic, oregano, chilli flakes and salt and pepper to taste, if using, in a large, shallow dish and mix well together.

2. Slice the chicken across the grain into 2.5-cm/1-inch thick slices. Toss in the marinade to coat. Cover and chill for 2–3 hours, turning occasionally.

3. Drain the chicken and discard the marinade. Heat a ridged griddle pan until hot. Add the chicken and cook over a medium–high heat for 3–4 minutes on each side. Cut into the thickest part of the meat to check that there are no remaining traces of pink or red. Transfer to a warmed plate.

4. Add the red peppers skin-side down to the pan and cook for 2 minutes on each side until cooked through. Transfer to the plate with the chicken.

5. Divide the chicken and red peppers between the tortillas, top with a little shredded lettuce, wrap and serve immediately.

CHILLI-PRAWN TACOS

SERVES: *4–6* | **PREP:** *15 mins* | **COOK:** *40 mins*

INGREDIENTS

600 g/1 lb 5 oz raw prawns, peeled
  and deveined
2 tbsp chopped fresh flat-leaf
  parsley
12 tortilla shells
4–6 lemon wedges, to serve

TACO SAUCE

1 tbsp olive oil
1 onion, finely chopped
1 green pepper, deseeded and diced
1–2 fresh hot green chillies, such
  as jalapeño, deseeded and finely
  chopped
3 garlic cloves, crushed
1 tsp ground cumin
1 tsp ground coriander
1 tsp brown sugar
450 g/1 lb ripe tomatoes, peeled
  and roughly chopped
juice of ½ lemon
salt and pepper (optional)

1. To make the taco sauce, heat the oil in a deep frying pan over a medium heat. Add the onion and cook for 5 minutes, or until soft. Add the green pepper and chillies and cook for 5 minutes. Add the garlic, cumin, coriander and sugar and cook for a further 2 minutes, stirring constantly.

2. Preheat the oven to 180°C/350°F/Gas Mark 4. Add the tomatoes, lemon juice and salt and pepper to taste, if using, to the sauce. Bring to the boil, then reduce the heat and simmer for 10 minutes. Stir in the prawns and parsley, cover and cook gently for 5–8 minutes, or until the prawns are pink and tender.

3. Meanwhile, place the tortilla shells, open-side down, on a baking sheet. Warm in the preheated oven for 2–3 minutes. Spoon the prawn mixture into the tortilla shells and serve immediately with the lemon wedges.

GREENS, PEA
& BEAN BURGERS

SERVES: *8* | **PREP:** *30 mins, plus standing* | **COOK:** *25 mins*

INGREDIENTS

115 g/4 oz peppery salad leaves,
such as rocket, mustard greens,
pak choi (green part only) or a
mixture, thick stems removed
60 g/2¼ oz cooked peas, mashed
400 g/14 oz canned butter beans,
drained, rinsed and mashed
1 tbsp grated onion
1½ tbsp chopped fresh mint
1 egg, beaten
40 g/1½ oz stale breadcrumbs
3 tbsp vegetable oil
salt and pepper (optional)

TO SERVE

4 oval pittas, halved crossways
16 cherry tomatoes, halved
8 tbsp mayonnaise

1. Roughly slice the salad leaves. Place in a steamer and steam for 3 minutes, then drain and rinse under cold running water, squeezing out as much liquid as possible.

2. Combine the cooked greens with the peas, beans, onion, mint, egg and salt and pepper, if using. Mix thoroughly with a fork. Stir in the breadcrumbs, mixing well to combine. Leave to stand at room temperature for 30 minutes.

3. Divide the mixture into eight 1-cm/½-inch thick patties, each 6 cm/2½ inches in diameter, firming the edges well.

4. Heat the oil in a non-stick frying pan over a medium–high heat. Working in batches, add the patties and fry for 2½–3 minutes on each side, turning carefully, until golden and crisp. Meanwhile, preheat the grill to medium.

5. Toast the pitta halves under the preheated grill. Stuff each half with a bean patty, cherry tomato halves and a dollop of mayonnaise. Serve immediately.

SALMON
QUINOA BURGERS

SERVES: *4* | **PREP:** *15 mins, plus chilling* | **COOK:** *20–25 mins*

INGREDIENTS

125 g/4½ oz quinoa

*275 g/9¾ oz cooked salmon, broken
    into flakes*

1 egg, beaten

4 spring onions, trimmed and sliced

1 tbsp chopped fresh coriander

4 wholemeal burger buns

1 tbsp olive oil, for frying

25 g/1 oz fresh watercress sprigs

¼ cucumber, sliced

salt and pepper (optional)

4 lime wedges, to serve

SPICY MAYONNAISE

2 tbsp capers, chopped

4 tbsp mayonnaise

juice of ½ lime

1. Bring a large saucepan of water to the boil. Add the quinoa, bring back to the boil and cook for 8–10 minutes. Drain well.

2. Place the quinoa in a bowl with the salmon, egg, spring onions and coriander. Season to taste with salt and pepper, if using, and mix well to combine.

3. With your hands, shape the mixture into four patties. Place them on a plate and chill in the refrigerator for 20 minutes.

4. Meanwhile, make the spicy mayonnaise. Mix the capers, mayonnaise and lime juice together in a small bowl. Set aside.

5. Halve and toast the burger buns.

6. Heat the oil in a frying pan, add the patties and cook over a medium heat for 4–5 minutes on each side until golden.

7. Spread the spicy mayonnaise over the bottom halves of the burger buns. Add a few sprigs of watercress and some slices of cucumber. Top with the patties and sandwich with the remaining bun halves.

8. Serve the burgers with lime wedges.

ROASTED MEDITERRANEAN VEGETABLE PIZZAS

SERVES: *4* | **PREP:** *50 mins, plus rising* | **COOK:** *30 mins*

INGREDIENTS

500 g/1 lb 2 oz plum tomatoes,
* halved*
1 red onion, cut into 8 wedges
1 aubergine, halved and sliced
1 red pepper, deseeded and
* quartered*
1 orange pepper, deseeded and
* quartered*
2 small courgettes, sliced
3 tbsp virgin olive oil, plus extra
* to serve*
1 tbsp basil leaves, plus extra
* to garnish*
2 tsp aged balsamic vinegar
175 g/6 oz goat's cheese, crumbled
sea salt flakes and pepper
* (optional)*

PIZZA BASES

250 g/9 oz wholemeal plain flour,
* plus extra for dusting*
½ tsp sea salt
1 tsp dark muscovado sugar
1 tsp easy-blend dried yeast
1 tbsp virgin olive oil
150–175 ml/5–6 fl oz lukewarm
* water*

1. Preheat the oven to 220°C/425°F/Gas Mark 7. To make the pizza bases, put the flour, salt, sugar and yeast in a mixing bowl and stir. Add the oil, then gradually mix in enough of the water to make a soft but not sticky dough.

2. Turn out the dough onto a work surface lightly dusted with flour and knead for 5 minutes until smooth and elastic. Return to the bowl, cover with a clean tea towel and leave to stand in a warm place for 45 minutes, or until doubled in size.

3. Arrange the tomatoes and red onion on a baking sheet in a single layer. Arrange the aubergine and peppers, cut-side down, on a second baking sheet in a single layer. Arrange the courgettes on a third baking sheet in a single layer. Drizzle with a little oil and sprinkle with salt and pepper, if using. Roast in the preheated oven for 15 minutes, then take out the courgettes. Roast the remaining trays for a further 5 minutes. Wrap the peppers in foil and leave to cool, then cut into slices.

4. Remove and discard the tomato skins, if liked, then chop the tomatoes, onion and basil and mix with the vinegar.

5. Lightly flour two baking sheets. Knead the dough, cut it into two pieces and roll out each piece into a 30-cm/12-inch x 15-cm/6-inch oval. Transfer to the prepared baking sheets, spoon over the tomato mixture, then top with the roasted vegetables. Leave to rise for 15 minutes.

6. Sprinkle the goat's cheese over the pizzas, then bake for 10 minutes, or until the bases are cooked and the cheese has melted. Sprinkle with oil and basil leaves, cut into wedges and serve.

FISH CAKES

INGREDIENTS

450 g/1 lb floury potatoes, cut into
chunks
450 g/1 lb mixed fish fillets, such as
cod and salmon, skinned
2 tbsp fresh tarragon
grated rind of 1 lemon
2 tbsp double cream
1 tbsp plain flour
1 egg, beaten
115 g/4 oz breadcrumbs, made
from day-old white bread or
wholemeal bread
4 tbsp vegetable oil, for shallow-
frying
salt and pepper (optional)
watercress, to serve
lemon wedges, to serve

1. Add 1–2 teaspoons of salt to a large saucepan of water and bring to the boil. Add the potatoes, bring back to the boil and cook for 15–20 minutes. Drain well and mash with a potato masher until smooth.

2. Put the fish in a frying pan and just cover with water. Place over a medium heat and bring to the boil, then reduce the heat, cover and simmer gently for 5 minutes until cooked.

3. Remove from the heat and transfer the fish to a plate using a slotted spoon. When cool enough to handle, flake the fish into large chunks, ensuring that there are no bones.

4. Mix the potatoes with the fish, tarragon, lemon rind and cream. Season to taste with salt and pepper, if using, and shape into four large patties or eight smaller ones.

5. Dust the patties with flour and dip them in the beaten egg. Coat thoroughly in the breadcrumbs. Place on a baking tray and chill in the refrigerator for at least 30 minutes.

6. Heat the oil in the frying pan, add the patties and fry over a medium heat for 5 minutes on each side, turning them carefully using a palette knife or a fish slice.

7. Serve with watercress, accompanied by lemon wedges for squeezing over the fish cakes.

HOME-MADE FISH FINGERS WITH CHILLI MAYONNAISE

SERVES: *4* | **PREP:** *20 mins* | **COOK:** *10 mins*

INGREDIENTS

200 g/7 oz plain flour
140 g/5 oz matzo meal
*450 g/1 lb firm white fish fillets, cut
  into strips*
3 eggs, beaten
*sunflower oil or groundnut oil, for
  shallow-frying*
salt and pepper (optional)

CHILLI MAYONNAISE

2 tbsp sweet chilli sauce
4–5 tbsp mayonnaise

1. Mix the flour with some salt and pepper to taste, if using, on a large flat plate.

2. Spread out the matzo meal on a separate flat plate.

3. Dip the fish pieces into the seasoned flour, then into the beaten egg, then into the matzo meal, coating generously.

4. Pour the oil into a non-stick frying pan to a depth of 1 cm/½ inch and heat. Add the fish pieces in batches and cook for a few minutes, turning once, until golden and cooked through.

5. To make the chilli mayonnaise, put the chilli sauce and mayonnaise in a bowl and beat together until combined.

6. Transfer the fish to warmed plates and serve with the chilli mayonnaise on the side.

TUNA-STUFFED AVOCADOS

INGREDIENTS

2 avocados

juice and grated rind of 1 lemon

juice and grated rind of 1 lime

1 tbsp sesame oil

350 g/12 oz canned tuna, drained and flaked

2 tbsp chopped fresh coriander

salt and pepper (optional)

1 tsp sesame seeds, to garnish

1. Using a sharp knife, cut through the avocados lengthways. Gently twist apart the halves and remove the stones.

2. Scoop out 2 tablespoons of the flesh from each avocado half and put it into a bowl. Add the lemon juice, lime juice and oil and mash well with a fork until smooth. Stir in the tuna and lemon rind and season to taste with salt and pepper, if using.

3. Pile the mixture into the avocado hollows and sprinkle with the grated lime rind and coriander. Garnish with a sprinkling of sesame seeds and serve.

TURKEY SAUSAGE PATTIES WITH MUSHROOMS & TOMATOES

SERVES: *4* | **PREP:** *15–20 mins* | **COOK:** *15 mins*

INGREDIENTS

400 g/14 oz fresh turkey mince

1 tsp dried thyme

1 tsp dried sage

½ tsp ground allspice

3 garlic cloves, crushed

4 tbsp oatmeal

1 small egg, beaten

3 tsp light olive oil

400 g/14 oz chestnut mushrooms, sliced

4 tomatoes, cut into wedges

salt and pepper (optional)

1. Combine the turkey with the thyme, sage, allspice, garlic, oatmeal, egg and salt and pepper to taste, if using, in a bowl. (The mixture can be stored, covered, in the refrigerator for up to 12 hours.)

2. Shape the mixture into eight small patties. Heat 2 teaspoons of the oil in a non-stick frying pan, add the patties and fry over a medium heat for a 4 minutes on each side, or until golden and cooked through with no pink inside. Transfer to a plate and keep warm.

3. Add the mushrooms to the pan and stir for 1 minute until soft. Pour in the remaining oil, then add the tomatoes and cook, without stirring, for a further 1–2 minutes to warm through. Serve the patties with the mushrooms and tomatoes.

BEEF & VEGETABLE KEBABS

MAKES: *20* | **PREP:** *25 mins, plus marinating, and soaking* | **COOK:** *15 mins, plus resting*

INGREDIENTS

juice of 1 lemon

2 tsp ground cumin

2 tsp ground coriander

2 tsp ground cinnamon

½ tsp cayenne pepper

2 garlic cloves, crushed

2 tbsp olive oil

600 g/1 lb 5 oz sirloin steak,
trimmed of fat and cut into
2-cm/¾-inch cubes

200 g/7 oz chestnut or button
mushrooms, halved or quartered,
if large

1 large red onion, cut into 2-cm/
¾-inch chunks

1 red pepper, deseeded and cut into
2-cm/¾-inch chunks

1 tsp sea salt flakes (optional)

1 tbsp fresh coriander leaves, to
garnish

1. Put the lemon juice, cumin, ground coriander, cinnamon, cayenne pepper, garlic and oil into a large bowl and stir well. Add the steak, mushrooms, onion and red pepper and mix well. Cover and marinate in the refrigerator for at least 2 hours, or overnight.

2. When you are ready to cook the kebabs, soak 20 wooden skewers in water for 20 minutes, then drain well. Preheat the oven to 230°C/450°F/Gas Mark 8. Line two baking trays with foil.

3. Thread the steak onto the skewers, alternating with the vegetables, and place them on the prepared baking trays. Sprinkle with the salt, if using. Roast in the preheated oven for 10 minutes for medium-rare or 12 minutes for medium, then cut into a steak cube to check it is done to your liking.

4. Leave the skewers to rest for 5 minutes under foil. Sprinkle with the fresh coriander and serve.

CHAPTER FOUR

DINNER

MUSHROOM & AUBERGINE MOUSSAKA

SERVES: *6* | **PREP:** *40 mins* | **COOK:** *1 hour 20 mins–1 hour 30 mins, plus cooling*

INGREDIENTS

3 large aubergines, thinly sliced
lengthways
2 tbsp olive oil
salt, for sprinkling

MUSHROOM SAUCE

2 tbsp olive oil
2 onions, finely chopped
2 garlic cloves, finely chopped
600 g/1 lb 5 oz mixed chestnut and
Portobello mushrooms, finely
chopped
5 fresh sage leaves, finely chopped
5 fresh thyme sprigs, leaves only
2 fresh oregano sprigs, chopped
½ tsp ground cinnamon
800 g/1 lb 12 oz canned chopped
tomatoes
100 ml/3½ fl oz water

BÉCHAMEL SAUCE

500 ml/17 fl oz milk
25 g/1 oz butter
40 g/1½ oz plain flour
¼ tsp freshly grated nutmeg
40 g/1½ oz freshly grated Parmesan
cheese
1 egg, lightly beaten
pepper (optional)

1. Preheat the oven to 200°C/400°F/Gas Mark 6. Line two baking trays with baking paper. Lay the aubergine slices on the prepared trays, brush them on both sides with the oil and sprinkle with salt. Roast in the preheated oven for 20 minutes, or until soft.

2. Meanwhile, to make the mushroom sauce, heat the oil in a frying pan over a low heat. Add the onions and garlic and fry for 10 minutes, or until soft. Stir in the mushrooms and fry for 5 minutes. Stir in the sage, thyme, oregano and cinnamon and fry for 2 minutes. Add the tomatoes and water. Bring to the boil, then reduce the heat to medium–low and simmer, partially covered, for 20 minutes.

3. To make the béchamel sauce, heat the milk in a saucepan until just below boiling point. Meanwhile, heat the butter in a saucepan over a medium–low heat until it starts to foam. Add the flour to the butter and stir constantly for 2 minutes until the mixture is smooth and comes away cleanly from the sides of the pan. Pour in the hot milk, a little at a time, stirring well between each addition to prevent lumps forming, until you have a thick, smooth sauce. Increase the heat to medium–high and bring the sauce to the boil, stirring constantly. Cook for a further 3 minutes, then stir in the nutmeg and season with pepper, if using. Remove from the heat and stir in the cheese. Leave to cool, then whisk in the egg.

4. To assemble the moussaka, put a layer of aubergine in the base of a lasagne dish, spread a third of the mushroom sauce on top, then add another layer of aubergine and a further third of the mushroom sauce. Repeat with a final layer of both. Spread the béchamel sauce evenly over the top. Bake for 30–35 minutes, or until golden and puffed up. Leave to cool for 10–15 minutes before serving.

LENTIL & MUSHROOM PIE

SERVES: 6 | **PREP:** 30–40 mins | **COOK:** 45–60 mins

INGREDIENTS

3 tbsp olive oil

1 fennel bulb, trimmed and thinly
    sliced

1 carrot, diced

1 celery stick, diced

1 shallot, chopped

6 garlic cloves, chopped

500 g/1 lb 2 oz chestnut
    mushrooms, thickly sliced

275 ml/9 fl oz vegetable stock

800 g/1 lb 12 oz canned green
    lentils, drained and rinsed

800 g/1 lb 12 oz canned chopped
    tomatoes

2 tsp dried thyme

1 tsp soft light brown sugar

4 tbsp finely chopped fresh parsley

salt and pepper (optional)

POTATO TOPPING

300 g/10½ oz sweet potatoes,
    chopped

600 g/1 lb 5 oz floury potatoes,
    chopped

25 g/1 oz butter, melted

salt (optional)

1. Preheat the oven to 200°C/400°F/Gas Mark 6.

2. Heat the oil in a saucepan over a medium heat. Add the fennel, carrot, celery and shallot, and fry, stirring occasionally, for 8–10 minutes until soft. Add the garlic and mushrooms, season to taste with salt, if using, and continue stirring for 5–8 minutes until the mushrooms are tender and have re-absorbed any liquid.

3. Stir the stock, lentils, tomatoes, thyme and sugar into the pan, with pepper to taste, if using. Bring to the boil and boil for 5–8 minutes, or until the liquid has evaporated. Stir in the parsley.

4. Meanwhile, make the potato topping. Add 1–2 teaspoons of salt, if using, to a large saucepan of water and bring to the boil. Add the sweet potatoes and boil for 5 minutes. Add the white potatoes and boil for a further 10 minutes, or until tender. Drain well and return to the pan over a low heat to steam dry. Use a wooden spoon to beat the potatoes.

5. Spoon the filling into a 30-cm/12-inch oval pie dish, or a 1.7-litre/3-pint ovenproof serving dish. Spoon the potatoes over the filling, smooth the surface and run a fork over it. Drizzle the butter over the potatoes and bake in the preheated oven for 20–25 minutes until the filling is bubbling. Place under a preheated grill for 3–5 minutes if you want the topping to brown. Serve immediately.

ASPARAGUS & SUN-DRIED TOMATO RISOTTO

INGREDIENTS

1 tbsp olive oil

40 g/1½ oz butter

1 small onion, finely chopped

6 sun-dried tomatoes, thinly sliced

280 g/10 oz risotto rice

1.2 litres/2 pints vegetable stock

225 g/8 oz fresh asparagus spears, cooked

85 g/3 oz freshly grated Parmesan cheese, plus extra to garnish

salt and pepper (optional)

lemon rind, to garnish

1. Heat the oil with 25 g/1 oz of the butter in a deep saucepan over a medium heat until the butter has melted.

2. Stir in the onion and sun-dried tomatoes and cook, stirring occasionally, for 5 minutes until the onion is soft and starting to turn golden. Do not brown.

3. Reduce the heat, add the rice and mix to coat in oil and butter. Cook, stirring constantly, for 2–3 minutes, or until the grains are translucent.

4. Gradually add the hot stock, a ladleful at a time. Stir constantly, adding more liquid as the rice absorbs each addition. Increase the heat to medium so that the liquid bubbles. Cook for 20 minutes, or until all the liquid is absorbed and the rice is creamy. Season to taste with salt and pepper, if using.

5. Meanwhile, cut most of the asparagus into 2.5-cm/1-inch pieces, reserving several whole spears to garnish. Carefully fold the asparagus into the risotto for the last 5 minutes of cooking time.

6. Remove the risotto from the heat and add the remaining butter. Mix well, then stir in the cheese until it melts.

7. Spoon the risotto into individual warmed serving dishes and garnish with the reserved asparagus spears. Sprinkle some cheese and lemon rind over the risotto and serve immediately.

BEAN & TOMATO CASSEROLE
WITH PARMESAN TOASTS

SERVES: *4* | **PREP:** *15–20 mins* | **COOK:** *1 hour 45 mins–2 hours*

INGREDIENTS

350 g/12 oz borlotti beans, soaked
  overnight
4 tbsp extra virgin olive oil, plus
  extra for drizzling
25 g/1 oz butter
1 large onion, thinly sliced
15–20 fresh sage leaves, sliced
2 large garlic cloves, finely chopped
1 tbsp tomato purée
800 g/1 lb 12 oz canned chopped
  tomatoes
300 ml/10 fl oz vegetable stock
4 tbsp chopped fresh flat-leaf parsley
50 g/1¾ oz freshly grated Parmesan
  cheese
8 slices ciabatta, toasted
sea salt and pepper (optional)
small fresh sage sprigs, to garnish

1. Drain the beans, rinse well and put into a large saucepan. Cover with water and bring to the boil. Boil for 10 minutes, then reduce the heat and simmer for 45 minutes–1 hour, or until tender. Drain.

2. Heat the oil and butter in a large saucepan over a medium heat. Add the onion and sage and fry for 5 minutes until the onion is translucent. Add the garlic and fry for 2 minutes until just coloured.

3. Add the tomato purée and fry for 1 minute, stirring.

4. Stir in the tomatoes, beans and stock and season to taste with salt and pepper, if using. Bring to the boil, then reduce the heat and simmer, partially covered, for 20 minutes. Add the parsley and half the cheese.

5. Ladle the beans into shallow soup plates. Top each plate with 2 slices of toasted ciabatta. Drizzle the bread with oil and sprinkle with the remaining cheese.

6. Garnish with sage sprigs and serve immediately.

VEGETABLE WELLINGTON

SERVES: *6* | **PREP:** *40 mins* | **COOK:** *1 hour 10 mins–1 hour 30 mins, plus standing*

INGREDIENTS

½ tsp saffron threads

200 g/7 oz long-grain rice

250 g/9 oz onions, thinly sliced

3 tbsp sunflower oil

40 g/1½ oz soft light brown sugar

500 g/1 lb 2 oz butternut squash,
    deseeded and cut into
    1-cm/½-inch pieces

2 tsp chilli oil

40 g/1½ oz butter

2 tsp olive oil

3 shallots, thinly sliced

4 garlic cloves, finely chopped

600 g/1 lb 5 oz mixed mushrooms,
    trimmed and finely chopped

2 x 225-g/8-oz rolled puff pastry
    sheets

3 tsp snipped fresh chives

125 g/4½ oz soft goat's cheese, cut
    into small pieces

1 egg, beaten

1. Preheat the oven to 200°C/400°F/Gas Mark 6. Bring a large saucepan of water to the boil with the saffron. Add the rice and boil for 10–12 minutes, or until tender. Drain well and leave to cool completely.

2. Meanwhile, toss the onions with the sunflower oil and sugar. Spread the onion mixture in a shallow roasting tin. Toss the butternut squash with the chilli oil and place in a separate shallow roasting tin. Roast the onion and squash in the preheated oven for 20–25 minutes, stirring frequently, until the onions are caramelized and the squash is tender. Leave both to cool completely.

3. Melt the butter with the olive oil in a large frying pan over a medium heat. Add the shallots and garlic and fry for 3–5 minutes. Stir in the mushrooms, increase the heat to high and fry for 12–15 minutes. Leave to cool completely.

4. Line a baking sheet with greaseproof paper. Cut one sheet of pastry into a 28 x 18-cm/11 x 7-inch rectangle. Spread half the rice over it, leaving a 1-cm/½-inch border.

5. Toss the squash, mushrooms and onions together, then stir in the chives and cheese. Spread the mixture over the pastry and top with the remaining rice. Brush the border with the beaten egg.

6. Lay the remaining pastry over the rice and press it onto the border. Trim the excess and press the edges together with a fork. Glaze with beaten egg. Cut four slashes in the top and bake in the preheated oven, for 20–25 minutes. Leave to stand for 10 minutes, then serve.

FISH & CHIPS

SERVES: *4* | **PREP:** *20 mins* | **COOK:** *20 mins*

INGREDIENTS

1 egg, beaten

*60 g/2¼ oz dried wholemeal
    breadcrumbs*

2 tsp seasoned salt

*4 skinless cod loin fillets, each
    weighing about 140 g/5 oz*

*600 g/1 lb 5 oz large floury potatoes,
    scrubbed and cut into chunky
    chips*

1 tsp garam masala

1 tsp paprika

½ tsp salt

1 tbsp groundnut oil

5 sprays cooking spray

320 g/11 oz frozen peas

SAUCE

2 tbsp mayonnaise

1 tbsp Greek-style natural yogurt

2 tsp lemon juice

1. Preheat the oven to 200°C/400°F/Gas Mark 6. Put the egg in a shallow dish. Put the breadcrumbs in a separate shallow dish and thoroughly stir in the seasoned salt. Dry the fish on kitchen paper.

2. Dry the potato chips on kitchen paper. Put them into a large bowl and stir in the garam masala, paprika, salt and oil. Combine thoroughly, then spread out the chips on a baking tray. Bake on the top shelf of the preheated oven for 5 minutes.

3. Meanwhile, dip each fish fillet in the beaten egg, allowing any excess to drip back into the dish, and then coat with the breadcrumbs. Place the fillets on a separate baking tray lined with baking paper and spray thoroughly with cooking spray.

4. Put the fish in the oven on the shelf beneath the chips and bake for 5 minutes. Turn the chips with a large spatula and return to the oven for a further 10 minutes, or until the chips are crisp on the outside and soft in the centre and the fish is cooked through.

5. Meanwhile, bring a small saucepan of water to the boil, add the peas and cook for 5 minutes, or until tender. Drain and keep warm.

6. To make the sauce, combine the mayonnaise, yogurt and lemon juice in a small bowl.

7. Serve the fish and chips immediately with the peas and sauce.

TUNA & BROCCOLI PASTA BAKE

INGREDIENTS

240 g/8½ oz dried wholemeal
penne pasta
200 g/7 oz broccoli florets
320 g/11 oz canned tuna steak in
olive oil, drained, 1½ tablespoons
of the oil reserved
1 tbsp red pesto
350 g/12 oz passata with onions
and garlic
6 cherry tomatoes, halved
100 g/3½ oz soft cheese
50 g/1¾ oz Cheddar cheese, grated
25 g/1 oz fresh wholemeal
breadcrumbs
salt (optional)
200 g/7 oz mixed salad leaves,
to serve

1. Preheat the oven to 190°C/375°F/Gas Mark 5. Add 1–2 teaspoons of salt, if using, to a large saucepan of water and bring to the boil. Add the pasta, bring back to the boil and cook for 12 minutes, or until tender but still firm to the bite. Drain.

2. Meanwhile, place the broccoli florets in a steamer and steam until just tender.

3. Flake the tuna. Put the reserved tuna oil, pesto and passata in a saucepan and cook, stirring, over a medium–high heat for 1–2 minutes until warmed through.

4. Tip the cooked pasta into a shallow ovenproof dish along with the sauce, broccoli, cherry tomatoes and tuna. Stir gently until all the pasta is well covered.

5. Dot the top with the soft cheese, then sprinkle over the Cheddar cheese and breadcrumbs. Bake in the preheated oven for 20 minutes, or until heated through and the cheese is golden and melted. Serve immediately with the salad leaves.

MONKFISH & PURPLE SPROUTING BROCCOLI COCONUT CURRY

SERVES: *4* | **PREP:** *20 mins* | **COOK:** *20 mins*

INGREDIENTS

1 large onion, chopped

2 tsp Thai fish sauce

juice of ½ lime

1 red chilli, de-stalked

1 green chilli, de-stalked

2 tsp crushed coriander seeds

2 tsp crushed cumin seeds

2.5-cm/1-inch piece fresh ginger, chopped

3 garlic cloves, roughly chopped

½ lemon grass stalk

1½ tbsp groundnut oil

5 curry leaves

300 ml/10 fl oz coconut milk

350 g/12 oz purple sprouting broccoli, each spear cut into 2 pieces

500 g/1 lb 2 oz monkfish fillet, cubed

1 red chilli, chopped, to garnish

1. Add the onion, fish sauce, lime juice, de-stalked chillies, coriander seeds, cumin seeds, ginger, garlic, lemon grass and half the oil to the bowl of a food processor and process to a paste. Tip the mixture into a frying pan and cook over a medium heat for 2 minutes. Stir in the curry leaves and coconut milk and simmer for a further 10 minutes.

2. Meanwhile, add the remaining oil to a separate frying pan and place over a high heat. Add the broccoli and stir-fry for 2 minutes, or until just tender. Set aside.

3. Add the monkfish cubes to the curry pan and bring back to a simmer. Cook for 2 minutes, then add the broccoli spears and continue cooking for a further 1 minute. Serve the curry with chopped red chilli sprinkled over the top.

FISH & POTATO
STEW

SERVES: *4* | **PREP:** *25 mins* | **COOK:** *45–50 mins*

INGREDIENTS

1½ tbsp olive oil, plus extra for
brushing
1 onion, finely chopped
3 large garlic cloves, 2 chopped and
1 halved
1 tbsp fennel seeds
½ tsp dried chilli flakes, or to taste
pinch of saffron threads
400 g/14 oz canned chopped
tomatoes
125 ml/4 fl oz fish stock or water
2 bay leaves
500 g/1 lb 2 oz floury potatoes,
thinly sliced
900 g/2 lb mixed fish, such as
hake, monkfish and red snapper,
skinned and cut into chunks
2 red peppers, deseeded and sliced
2 tbsp fresh flat-leaf parsley
salt and pepper (optional)

1. Preheat the oven to 180°C/350°F/Gas Mark 4.

2. Heat the oil in a saucepan over a medium heat. Add the onion and fry, stirring, for 2 minutes. Add the chopped garlic, fennel seeds, chilli flakes and saffron and fry for a further 1 minute, or until the onion is soft. Add the tomatoes, stock and bay leaves and season to taste with salt and pepper, if using. Cover and bring to the boil, then reduce the heat to very low and simmer for 10 minutes.

3. Meanwhile, rub the garlic halves all over a 1.5-litre/2½-pint baking dish, pressing down firmly, then set aside the dish, discarding the garlic. Add 1–2 teaspoons of salt, if using, to a large saucepan of water and bring to the boil. Add the potatoes, bring back to the boil and cook for 8–10 minutes, or until they are starting to soften but still hold their shape. Drain well, pat dry and set aside.

4. Place the prepared baking dish on a baking sheet and arrange half the potatoes in a layer on the base of the dish. Place the fish and red peppers on top. Spoon over the tomato sauce, sprinkle with the parsley and shake the dish slightly. Arrange the remaining potatoes on top to cover all the other ingredients and lightly brush with oil. Bake in the preheated oven for 20–25 minutes, or until the fish and potatoes are tender when pierced with a skewer. Serve immediately.

ROLLED STUFFED TURKEY BREAST

SERVES: *4–6* | **PREP:** *25–30 mins* | **COOK:** *55 mins–1 hour 10 mins, plus resting*

INGREDIENTS

1.6 kg/3 lb 8 oz boneless turkey breast, butterflied

4–6 slices Parma ham

1 tbsp olive oil

salt and pepper (optional)

SAUSAGE & PEPPER STUFFING

1 tbsp olive oil

200 g/7 oz spicy Italian sausage meat, crumbled

1 shallot, finely chopped

2 garlic cloves, chopped

100 g/3½ oz fine breadcrumbs

2 tbsp finely chopped fresh flat-leaf parsley

2 chargrilled red peppers in olive oil, drained and sliced

1. Preheat the oven to 190°C/375°F/Gas Mark 5. Open out the turkey and cover it with a sheet of clingfilm. Use a meat mallet or rolling pin to pound it into a rectangle no more than 1 cm/½ inch thick. Season to taste with salt and pepper, if using, cover with the ham slices, then set aside.

2. To make the stuffing, heat the oil in a large frying pan over a medium heat. Add the sausage meat and fry, stirring to break it up, for 3–5 minutes until brown and cooked through. Use a slotted spoon to remove the meat, leaving 1 tablespoon of oil in the pan.

3. Add the shallot to the pan and fry, stirring, for 1–2 minutes until starting to colour. Stir in the garlic and continue stirring for a further 1 minute. Add the breadcrumbs and season to taste with salt and pepper, if using. Stir in the parsley.

4. Place the turkey breast skin-side down on a work surface. Make a cut along the length of the breast, down the centre, without cutting all the way through. Mound the stuffing into the centre, then spread it over the top of the breast, leaving a 1-cm/½-inch border. Arrange the red pepper slices on top of the stuffing. Roll up the turkey Swiss-roll fashion. Use kitchen string to tie it in three or four places.

5. Add the oil to the pan and heat over a high heat. Add the turkey and fry for 3–5 minutes, or until golden brown. Transfer to a roasting tin and roast in the preheated oven for 35–40 minutes, or until the juices run clear. Transfer to a chopping board, cover with foil and leave to rest for 8–10 minutes before slicing and serving.

CHICKEN & BROCCOLI CASSEROLE

SERVES: *4* | **PREP:** *10 mins* | **COOK:** *35–40 mins*

INGREDIENTS

400 g/14 oz broccoli florets

40 g/1½ oz butter

1 onion, thinly sliced

350 g/12 oz cooked chicken, cut
*   into bite-sized chunks*

100 g/3½ oz crème fraîche

200 ml/7 fl oz chicken stock

25 g/1 oz fresh white breadcrumbs

55 g /2 oz Gruyère or Emmenthal
*   cheese, grated*

salt and pepper (optional)

1. Preheat the oven to 200°C/400°F/Gas Mark 6. Add 1–2 teaspoons of salt, if using, to a large saucepan of water and bring to the boil. Add the broccoli, bring back to the boil and cook for 5 minutes until tender. Drain well.

2. Meanwhile, melt 25 g/1 oz of the butter in a frying pan, add the onion and fry over a medium heat for 3–4 minutes until soft.

3. Layer the broccoli, onion and chicken in a 1.5-litre/2½-pint ovenproof dish and season to taste with salt and pepper, if using. Pour over the crème fraîche and stock.

4. Melt the remaining butter in a small saucepan and stir in the breadcrumbs. Mix with the cheese and sprinkle over the chicken mixture.

5. Place the dish on a baking sheet in the preheated oven and bake for 20–25 minutes until golden brown and bubbling. Serve hot.

ROAST CHICKEN WITH WATERCRESS BUTTER

SERVES: *4* | **PREP:** *30 mins* | **COOK:** *1 hour 50 mins, plus resting*

INGREDIENTS

85 g/3 oz watercress, leaves
stripped from the stalks
100 g/3½ oz unsalted butter, at
room temperature
finely grated rind and juice of
1 small orange
2 tbsp finely chopped shallots
½ tsp black peppercorns, crushed
large pinch of sea salt
1 chicken, weighing 1.5 kg/3 lb 5 oz
400 ml/14 fl oz chicken stock
2 tsp plain flour
salt and pepper (optional)

1. Preheat the oven to 200°C/400°F/Gas Mark 6.

2. Chop the watercress and mix with the butter, orange rind, shallots, peppercorns and sea salt.

3. Loosen the chicken skin by pushing your fingers underneath. Insert the watercress butter under the skin, smoothing it to the shape of the bird.

4. Place the chicken breast-side down in a roasting tin. Add 6–8 tablespoons of the stock, then transfer to the preheated oven and roast for 20 minutes.

5. Turn the chicken over and reduce the oven temperature to 180°C/350°F/Gas Mark 4. Roast for a further 1 hour 15 minutes, basting occasionally, until the juices run clear when a skewer is inserted into the thickest part of the meat. Transfer the chicken to a warmed serving platter and leave to rest for 10 minutes.

6. Pour away most of the fat from the tin. Sprinkle the juices with the flour and stir over a medium heat, scraping up the sediment from the base of the tin. Stir in the orange juice, the remaining stock and any juices that have flowed from the chicken. Bring to the boil, stirring. Check the seasoning, adding salt and pepper to taste, if using. Strain the gravy into a jug and serve immediately with the chicken.

BAKED
CHICKEN WINGS

SERVES: *4* | **PREP:** *15–20 mins* | **COOK:** *40–50 mins*

INGREDIENTS

2 tbsp plain flour

¼ tsp paprika

24 chicken wings, trimmed

2 tbsp olive oil

4 spicy Italian sausages, cut into
*   4-cm/1½-inch pieces*

1 onion, thinly sliced

2 red peppers, deseeded and sliced

4 pickled cherry peppers, sliced

4 garlic cloves, sliced

225 ml/8 fl oz chicken stock

2 tbsp lemon juice

salt and pepper (optional)

4 tbsp chopped fresh flat-leaf
*   parsley, to garnish*

1. Mix together the flour and paprika in a wide dish. Season the chicken wings with salt and pepper, if using, then dredge them in the flour mixture, shaking off the excess.

2. Heat the oil in a large, deep frying pan over a medium–high heat. Add as many chicken wings as will fit in the pan in a single layer, and fry for 3–5 minutes until golden brown on both sides. Remove from the pan and set aside. Add extra oil to the pan, if needed, and repeat until all the wings are fried.

3. Pour off all but 1 tablespoon of the oil from the pan. Add the sausages to the pan and fry for 3–5 minutes until brown all over. Remove from the pan and set aside.

4. Pour off all but 1 tablespoon of the oil from the pan. Add the onion and red peppers to the pan and stir for 3–5 minutes until soft. Add the cherry peppers and garlic and stir for a further 2 minutes until the garlic is soft.

5. Return the chicken and sausages to the pan. Stir in the stock and lemon juice and season to taste with salt and pepper, if using. Bring to the boil, cover the pan, reduce the heat to low and simmer for 15–20 minutes until the wings are cooked through and the juices run clear when you cut into one.

6. Using a slotted spoon, transfer the wings, sausages, red peppers and cherry peppers to warmed plates. Bring the liquid in the pan to the boil, then spoon it over the meat. Garnish with parsley and serve immediately.

CHICKEN
PARMESAN

SERVES: *4* | **PREP:** *15–20 mins* | **COOK:** *45–50 mins, plus standing*

INGREDIENTS

100 g/3½ oz plain flour

200 g/7 oz dry breadcrumbs

*4 skinless, boneless chicken breasts,
  250 g/9 oz each*

2 eggs, beaten

2 tbsp olive oil, plus extra if needed

250 g/9 oz mozzarella cheese, sliced

*125 g/4½ oz freshly grated
  Parmesan cheese*

salt and pepper (optional)

*1 tbsp chopped fresh flat-leaf
  parsley, to garnish*

SIMPLE MARINARA SAUCE

2 tbsp olive oil

1 large onion, chopped

2 large garlic cloves, chopped

1 tbsp dried mixed herbs

*800 g/1 lb 12 oz canned chopped
  tomatoes*

275 ml/9 fl oz passata

2 tsp dried oregano

pinch of sugar

salt and pepper (optional)

1. To make the sauce, heat the oil in a large saucepan. Add the onion and fry, stirring, for 2 minutes. Add the garlic and cook, stirring, until the onion is soft. Stir in the mixed herbs, tomatoes, passata, oregano and sugar and season to taste with salt and pepper, if using. Bring to the boil, then cover and simmer for 15 minutes. Transfer to a blender or food processor and process to a purée.

2. Meanwhile, preheat the oven to 200°C/400°F/Gas Mark 6. Spread the flour over a plate and put the breadcrumbs on a separate plate. Cut the chicken breasts in half horizontally.

3. Place the chicken pieces between sheets of clingfilm and pound with a meat mallet or rolling pin to a thickness of about 5 mm/ ¼ inch. Season both sides with salt and pepper, if using. Dust a chicken breast with flour, shaking off the excess, then dip in the egg to coat. Dip in the breadcrumbs to coat both sides, then set aside and repeat with the remaining chicken pieces.

4. Heat the oil in a frying pan over a medium–high heat. Add as many chicken pieces as will fit in the pan in a single layer and fry on each side for 2 minutes until golden. Drain on kitchen paper. Fry the remaining pieces, adding extra oil, if necessary. Pour half of the sauce into a baking dish that will hold the chicken in a single layer. Arrange the chicken on top, then pour over the remaining sauce. Arrange the mozzarella cheese on top and sprinkle over the Parmesan cheese. Bake in the preheated oven for 20–25 minutes, or until the cheese is melted, golden and bubbling. Leave to stand for 5 minutes, then garnish with parsley and serve immediately.

SESAME SOBA NOODLES
WITH GRILLED CHICKEN

SERVES: 4 | **PREP:** 25 mins, plus marinating | **COOK:** 20 mins

INGREDIENTS

juice and zest of 1 large orange

1 tbsp soft dark brown sugar

1 tbsp rice vinegar

1 tbsp soy sauce

1 garlic clove, finely chopped

1 tbsp finely chopped fresh ginger

450 g/1 lb boneless, skinless chicken
  breasts, cut into strips

350 g/12 oz dried soba noodles

115 g/4 oz sugar snap peas, halved
  crossways

6 small radishes, thinly sliced

4 spring onions, thinly sliced,
  to garnish

SESAME SAUCE

1 garlic clove, peeled

2.5-cm/1-inch piece fresh ginger,
  peeled

70 g/2½ oz tahini

2 tbsp soft dark brown sugar

2 tbsp soy sauce

2 tbsp sesame oil

1 tbsp rice vinegar

¼–½ tsp hot chilli oil

1–2 tbsp lukewarm water

1. Combine the orange juice and zest, sugar, vinegar, soy sauce, garlic and ginger in a medium-sized bowl. Add the chicken and toss to coat. Marinate for at least 30 minutes or overnight.

2. Cook the noodles according to the packet instructions. Drain and keep warm.

3. Preheat the grill to high. Remove the chicken strips from the marinade (discarding the marinade), and cook under the grill for about 4 minutes on each side until cooked through.

4. To make the sesame sauce, process the garlic and ginger in a blender or food processor until finely chopped. Add the tahini, sugar, soy sauce, sesame oil, vinegar and chilli oil and process until smooth. Add the water, a little at a time, until the desired consistency is achieved.

5. Pour the sauce over the warm noodles and toss to coat. Add the sugar snap peas and radishes and toss to combine. Serve the noodles topped with the strips of chicken and garnished with the spring onions.

SAUSAGES
& PEPPERS

SERVES: *4* | **PREP:** *15–20 mins* | **COOK:** *25–30 mins*

INGREDIENTS

4 tbsp olive oil

8 Italian sausages

1 large green pepper, deseeded and sliced

1 large red pepper, deseeded and sliced

2 onions, sliced

2 large garlic cloves, finely chopped

150 ml/5 fl oz passata

salt and pepper (optional)

1 tbsp basil leaves, to garnish

1. Heat the oil in a large frying pan with a tight-fitting lid over a medium heat. Add the sausages, in batches if necessary, and fry, stirring, until brown all over. Remove from the pan and set aside. Pour off all but 2 tablespoons of the fat from the pan.

2. Add the green pepper, red pepper and onions to the pan and cook, stirring, for 3 minutes until beginning to soften. Add the garlic and stir for a further 1 minute.

3. Add the passata and season to taste with salt and pepper, if using. Return the sausages to the pan and bring the mixture to the boil, stirring constantly.

4. Reduce the heat to very low, cover and simmer for 12–15 minutes until the sausages are cooked through and the peppers are tender. Adjust the seasoning, if using. Garnish with basil leaves and serve.

SPAGHETTI BOLOGNESE

SERVES: *4* | **PREP:** *15–20 mins* | **COOK:** *30–40 mins*

INGREDIENTS

2 tbsp olive oil

1 onion, finely chopped

2 garlic cloves, finely chopped

1 carrot, finely chopped

1 tsp dried oregano

½ tsp dried thyme

1 bay leaf

280 g/10 oz fresh lean beef mince

300 ml/10 fl oz stock

300 ml/10 fl oz passata

350 g/12 oz dried spaghetti

salt and pepper (optional)

1. Heat the oil in a heavy-based, non-stick saucepan. Add the onion and cook, half covered, for 5 minutes, or until soft. Add the garlic and carrot and cook for a further 3 minutes, stirring occasionally.

2. Add the oregano, thyme, bay leaf and mince to the pan and cook, stirring frequently, until the meat is brown all over.

3. Add the stock and passata. Reduce the heat, season to taste with salt and pepper, if using, and cook over a medium–low heat, half covered, for 15–20 minutes, or until the sauce has reduced and thickened. Remove and discard the bay leaf.

4. Meanwhile, add 1–2 tsp salt, if using, to a large saucepan of water and bring to the boil. Add the pasta, bring back to the boil and cook for 8–10 minutes until tender but still firm to the bite. Drain well and mix with the sauce until the pasta is well coated. Serve immediately.

BEEF BRISKET
WITH SOY & GINGER RUB

SERVES: 6–8 | **PREP:** *20 mins, plus marinating & standing* | **COOK:** *10 hours, plus resting*

INGREDIENTS

2 kg/4 lb 8 oz boneless brisket of beef

SOY & GINGER RUB

100 g/3½ oz soft light brown sugar
150 ml/5 fl oz soy sauce
150 ml/5 fl oz mirin
2 tbsp Korean chilli bean paste
4 garlic cloves, crushed
55 g/2 oz fresh ginger, sliced
1 tsp pepper
1 tsp Sichuan peppercorns
3 star anise
1 cinnamon stick

1. To make the rub, mix all the ingredients together in a large bowl. Add the beef and stir until thoroughly coated.

2. Place the beef in a tight-fitting non-metallic dish and pour over any remaining rub from the bowl. Cover with clingfilm and marinate in the refrigerator for at least 24 hours.

3. Remove the beef from the refrigerator at least 1 hour before you want to cook it to allow it to come to room temperature..

4. Prepare the barbecue for smoking and preheat to low. Place the beef on the barbecue rack, point side up, and smoke it with the lid on for 10 hours, or until the centre of the meat is no longer pink and the juices run clear.

5. Cover the beef with foil and leave to rest in a warm place before slicing and serving.

THIN RIBS IN A STICKY BARBECUE MARINADE

SERVES: 4 | **PREP:** 15 mins, plus marinating | **COOK:** 3 hours 10 mins, plus cooling

INGREDIENTS

2 kg/4 lb 8 oz beef short ribs

MARINADE

1 onion, finely chopped

2 garlic cloves, crushed

2 tbsp English mustard

1 tbsp smoked paprika

1 tbsp dried oregano

1 tbsp smoked chipotle sauce

1 tsp fennel seeds

100 ml/3½ fl oz light soy sauce

100 g/3½ oz dark muscovado sugar

100 ml/3½ fl oz tomato ketchup

100 ml/3½ fl oz cider vinegar

200 ml/7 fl oz water

1 tsp celery salt

1 tsp pepper

1. To make the marinade, place all the ingredients in a large non-metallic bowl and mix together.

2. Add the ribs to the marinade, cover and chill in the refrigerator for a minimum of 4 hours, or for up to 12 hours if time allows. Turn every couple of hours to coat.

3. Preheat the oven to 180°C/350°F/Gas Mark 4. Transfer the ribs and marinade to a large flameproof casserole with a tight-fitting lid. Cover and cook in the preheated oven for 3 hours.

4. Remove from the oven and leave to cool slightly, then remove the ribs from the sauce, set aside and keep warm. Skim any excess fat from the surface of the remaining marinade, then place the casserole over a medium heat and cook until reduced to a sticky consistency. Drizzle the reduced marinade over the ribs and serve.

CHILLI
CON CARNE

SERVES: *4* | **PREP:** *10 mins* | **COOK:** *20–25 mins*

INGREDIENTS

1 tbsp olive oil

500 g/1 lb 2 oz fresh beef mince

1 onion, chopped

2 red peppers, deseeded and sliced

2½ tsp chilli powder

400 g/14 oz canned red kidney beans, drained and rinsed

400 g/14 oz canned cannellini beans, drained and rinsed

400 g/14 oz canned chopped tomatoes

1 tbsp tomato purée

100 ml/3½ fl oz vegetable stock

200 g/7 oz basmati rice

2 tbsp chopped fresh coriander

2 tbsp soured cream

¼ tsp smoked paprika

salt and pepper (optional)

1. Heat the oil in a large frying pan, add the mince and cook for 2–3 minutes until brown all over.

2. Add the onion and red peppers and cook, stirring occasionally, for 3–4 minutes.

3. Stir in the chilli powder and cook for 1 minute, then add the kidney beans, cannellini beans, tomatoes, tomato purée and stock. Bring to a simmer and simmer for 12–15 minutes. Season to taste with salt and pepper, if using.

4. Meanwhile, cook the rice according to the packet instructions.

5. Stir the coriander into the chilli and serve in warmed bowls with the rice, topped with a dollop of soured cream and a sprinkling of smoked paprika.

MINTY LAMB MEATBALLS
WITH SOBA NOODLES

SERVES: *4* | **PREP:** *25 mins* | **COOK:** *15 mins*

INGREDIENTS

2 sprays of cooking spray, for
*   greasing*
450 g/1 lb fresh lamb mince
1 shallot, finely chopped
2 garlic cloves, finely chopped
1 tbsp fresh mint leaves, finely
*   chopped*
1 tbsp fresh coriander leaves, finely
*   chopped*
2 serrano chillies, deseeded and
*   chopped*
1 tbsp Thai fish sauce
75 g/2¾ oz panko breadcrumbs
1 egg
350 g/12 oz dried soba noodles
35 g/1¼ oz crushed dry-roasted
*   peanuts, to garnish*

PESTO

2 serrano chillies
2.5-cm/1-inch piece fresh ginger
4 garlic cloves
55 g/2 oz fresh mint leaves
10 g/¼ oz fresh basil leaves
juice of 1 lime
1 tbsp Thai fish sauce
1 tbsp sugar
3 tbsp vegetable oil

1. Preheat the oven to 200°C/400°F/Gas Mark 6. Line a large baking tray with baking paper and spray it with cooking spray.

2. Put the lamb, shallot, garlic, mint, coriander, chillies, fish sauce, breadcrumbs and egg into a bowl and mix well to combine. Shape the meat mixture into 4-cm/1½-inch balls and place them on the prepared tray. Lightly spritz the tops with cooking spray and bake in the preheated oven for 15 minutes, or until cooked through.

3. Meanwhile, to make the pesto, halve and deseed the chillies and peel and chop the ginger. Put them into a food processor with the garlic and process until finely chopped. Add the mint, basil, lime juice, fish sauce, sugar and oil and process to a smooth purée.

4. Cook the noodles according to the packet instructions. Drain and toss with the pesto in a large bowl. Serve immediately topped with the meatballs and garnished with the peanuts.

CHAPTER FIVE

DESSERTS & BAKING

BANANA SPLIT
LOLLIES

MAKES: 8 | **PREP:** 15 mins, plus freezing | **COOK:** 10 mins

INGREDIENTS

4 bananas

6 tbsp icing sugar

2 tbsp coconut cream

100 g/3½ oz vanilla yogurt

400 g/14 oz plain chocolate, roughly
  chopped

100 g/3½ oz sweetened desiccated
  coconut, to decorate

1. Peel the bananas. Put them in a blender with the icing sugar, coconut cream and yogurt and whizz until smooth. Pour the mixture into eight 60 ml/2 fl oz ice pop moulds. Insert the ice pop sticks and freeze for 4 hours, or until firm.

2. When the banana mixture is frozen, line a baking sheet with baking paper. To unmould the ice pops, dip the frozen moulds into warm water for a few seconds and gently release the pops while holding the sticks. Place them on the prepared baking sheet and return to the freezer for 1–2 hours.

3. Put the chocolate in a heatproof bowl set over a saucepan of gently simmering water and heat until melted. Remove from the heat and leave to cool slightly.

4. Dip each ice pop into the melted chocolate, then sprinkle over the desiccated coconut. Return to the prepared baking sheet and freeze for 10–20 minutes, or until ready to serve.

PISTACHIO
ICE CREAM

SERVES: *6* | **PREP:** *10 mins, plus freezing* | **COOK:** *No cooking*

INGREDIENTS

75 g/2¾ oz unsalted pistachio nuts, shelled
350 ml/12 fl oz coconut milk
350 ml/12 fl oz almond milk
8–10 Medjool dates, stoned
1 tsp vanilla extract
½ tsp almond extract

1. Put the nuts and about 125 ml/4 fl oz of the coconut milk into a food processor and process to a smooth paste.

2. Put the remaining coconut milk, the almond milk, dates, vanilla extract and almond extract into a blender. Whizz on high speed for 3–5 minutes until puréed. Add the pistachio paste and process until well combined.

3. Transfer the mixture to the chilled container of an electric ice-cream maker and freeze according to the manufacturer's instructions. The ice cream can be served immediately, or you can transfer it to a freezer-proof container and freeze overnight for a more solid consistency.

APPLE
PIE

SERVES: *6–8* | **PREP** *25 mins, plus chilling* | **COOK:** *50 mins*

INGREDIENTS

175 g /6 oz plain flour
pinch of salt
85 g/3 oz butter, cut into pieces
85 g/3 oz lard, cut into small pieces
1–2 tbsp water, plus extra
* for sealing*
beaten egg or milk, for glazing

FILLING

750 g/1 lb 10 oz cooking apples,
* peeled, cored and sliced*
125 g/4½ oz soft light brown sugar,
* plus extra for sprinkling*
½–1 tsp ground cinnamon

1. Sift together the flour and salt into a mixing bowl. Add the butter and lard and rub it in with your fingertips until the mixture resembles fine breadcrumbs.

2. Add enough water to mix to a firm dough. Wrap in clingfilm and chill in the refrigerator for 30 minutes.

3. Preheat the oven to 220°C/425°F/Gas Mark 7. Thinly roll out almost two thirds of the pastry and use to line a deep 23-cm/9-inch pie plate.

4. To make the filling, mix the apples with the sugar and cinnamon and pack into the pastry case.

5. Roll out the remaining pastry to make a lid. Dampen the edges of the pie rim with water and position the lid, pressing the edges firmly together. Trim and crimp the edges.

6. Use the pastry trimmings to cut out leaves or other shapes. Dampen and attach to the top of the pie.

7. Glaze the pie with beaten egg, then make one or two slits in the top and place the pie on a baking sheet.

8. Bake in the preheated oven for 20 minutes, then reduce the temperature to 180°C/350°F/Gas Mark 4 and bake for a further 30 minutes, or until the pastry is a light golden brown.

9. Sprinkle with sugar and serve hot or cold.

MINI
PECAN PIES

MAKES: *12* | **PREP:** *20 mins* | **COOK:** *20–25 mins*

INGREDIENTS

1 x 325 -g/11½ -oz sheet ready-
rolled shortcrust pastry
55 g/2 oz pecan nuts
25 g/1 oz butter, plus extra
for greasing
40 g/1½ oz light muscovado sugar
3 tbsp maple syrup
1 large egg
1 tsp vanilla extract
1 tbsp maple syrup, for glazing

1. Preheat the oven to 220°C/425°F/Gas Mark 7 and place a baking sheet in the oven. Lightly grease a shallow 12-hole bun tin. Unroll the pastry and use a 7-cm/2¾-inch round, fluted cutter to stamp out 12 rounds. Press each round into a hole in the prepared tin.

2. Roughly chop the nuts and divide between the pastry cases. Place the butter in a saucepan over a low heat and heat until just melted. Put the sugar, maple syrup, egg and vanilla extract into a bowl and whisk with a balloon whisk until combined. Whisk in the melted butter, then carefully pour the mixture into the pastry cases, taking care not to overfill.

3. Place the tin on the baking sheet in the preheated oven and bake for 15–17 minutes, or until the pastry is golden and the filling is just set. Lightly brush the hot pies with maple syrup. Serve warm or cold.

KEY LIME
POTS

SERVES: *4* | **PREP:** *10 mins* | **COOK:** *10 mins, plus chilling*

INGREDIENTS

275 ml/9 fl oz double cream
1½ tbsp rice malt syrup
25 g/1 oz plain chocolate, 85%
cocoa solids, broken into pieces
finely grated zest of 1 lime
1½ tbsp lime juice
1 tsp cocoa powder

1. Put the cream in a saucepan and slowly bring to the boil over a medium heat. Add the rice malt syrup and stir well, then boil for 3 minutes. Add the chocolate, most of the lime zest and all the lime juice, and cook, stirring, until the chocolate has melted.

2. Pour the mixture into four espresso cups. Cover with clingfilm and chill in the refrigerator for at least 4 hours.

3. Decorate the pots with the cocoa powder and remaining lime zest and serve.

RICE PUDDING WITH CINNAMON-POACHED PLUMS

SERVES: *4* | **PREP:** *15 mins* | **COOK:** *50–55 mins*

INGREDIENTS

85 g/3 oz pudding rice
25 g/1 oz caster sugar
15 g/½ oz unsalted butter
500 ml/17 fl oz milk
1 thinly pared strip of orange rind

COMPOTE

500 g/1 lb 2 oz red plums, stoned
 and halved
1 cinnamon stick
2 tbsp golden caster sugar
juice of 1 orange

1. Put the rice, sugar and butter into a saucepan and stir in the milk and orange rind. Heat over a medium heat, stirring occasionally, until almost boiling.

2. Reduce the heat to low, then cover and simmer for 40–45 minutes, stirring occasionally, until the rice is tender and most of the liquid has been absorbed.

3. Meanwhile, to make the compote, put the plums, cinnamon stick, sugar and orange juice into a large saucepan. Heat over a medium heat until just boiling, then reduce the heat to low, cover and simmer for about 10 minutes, or until the plums are tender.

4. Remove the plums with a slotted spoon and discard the cinnamon. Serve the rice pudding warm with the compote.

ROASTED FRUIT CRUMBLE

SERVES: *4* | **PREP:** *15 mins* | **COOK:** *35–40 mins*

INGREDIENTS

4 apricots, stoned and quartered

1 tbsp caster sugar

200 g/7 oz raspberries

200 g/7 oz blackberries

55 g/2 oz rolled oats

40 g/1½ oz wholemeal flour

25 g/1 oz pecan nuts

10 g/¼ oz sesame seeds

60 g/2¼ oz muscovado sugar

60 g/2¼ oz coconut oil

1. Preheat the oven to 180°C/350°F/Gas Mark 4.

2. Place the apricot quarters in a roasting tin and sprinkle with the sugar. Roast in the preheated oven for 15 minutes.

3. Spoon the apricots into four ovenproof dishes and sprinkle over the remaining fruit.

4. Place the remaining ingredients in a food processor and process until they resemble very lumpy breadcrumbs.

5. Spoon the crumble over the fruit, place the dishes on a baking sheet and bake in the oven for 20–25 minutes until golden and bubbling. Serve hot.

SUMMER PUDDINGS

SERVES: *6* | **PREP:** *25–30 mins* | **COOK:** *8–10 mins, plus chilling*

INGREDIENTS

*250 g/9 oz strawberries, hulled and
    halved*
250 g/9 oz raspberries
150 g/5½ oz redcurrants
100 g/3½ oz blueberries
200 g/7 oz caster sugar
1 tbsp lemon juice
1 tsp vanilla extract
18 thin slices wholemeal bread
200 g/7 oz crème fraîche, to serve

1. Set aside 12 strawberry halves and 18 raspberries for decoration.

2. Put the remaining berries in a saucepan with the sugar and a little water. Cook over a low heat, stirring occasionally, for 8–10 minutes, or until the berries have produced plenty of juice and have broken up a little without completely disintegrating. Remove from the heat and add the lemon juice and vanilla extract.

3. Line six 225–275-ml/8–9-fl oz ramekins with clingfilm, making sure the film is draped over the sides.

4. Cut out a round the diameter of a ramekin from each slice of bread (the leftover bread can be made into breadcrumbs for another recipe) and dip each slice into the fruit pan so one side is covered in juice. Use the bread and the berries to layer up each ramekin – put a little berry juice in the base of the ramekin first, followed by a bread slice (juice-covered side up) and 1–2 spoonfuls of the berries. Repeat the layers until all the berries and bread are used up, finishing each dessert with a bread slice on top (juice-covered side up).

5. Put the ramekins on a tray and cover the top of each with a small saucer, then place a heavy weight, such as a bag of dried beans, on top of each. Chill in the refrigerator overnight, or until ready to serve.

6. Turn out the puddings onto plates and decorate with the reserved fruit. Top each pudding with a generous spoonful of crème fraîche and serve immediately.

MELTING CHOCOLATE RISOTTO

SERVES: *4–6* | **PREP:** *10 mins* | **COOK:** *45 mins, plus resting*

INGREDIENTS

400 ml/14 fl oz milk

25 g/1 oz caster sugar

100 g/3½ oz arborio rice

1 tsp vanilla extract

100 g/3½ oz plain chocolate,
  broken into small pieces

4–6 tbsp double cream

1. Preheat the oven to 150°C/300°F/Gas Mark 2. Place a 1-litre/ 1¾-pint ovenproof dish in the oven to warm through.

2. Put the milk, sugar and rice into a saucepan and bring just to the boil over a low heat.

3. Stir through the vanilla extract and 75 g/2¾ oz of the chocolate and stir until the chocolate has melted. Carefully transfer to the dish to the preheated oven. Cover with foil and bake for 30 minutes.

4. Remove from the oven, stir well, re-cover and leave to rest for 5 minutes. Drizzle over the cream and swirl it into the risotto. Scatter with the remaining chocolate to serve.

APPLE &
OATMEAL COOKIES

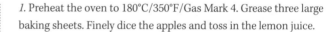

MAKES: *26* | **PREP:** *20 mins* | **COOK:** *12–15 mins*

INGREDIENTS

2 large apples, peeled and cored,
  200 g/7 oz unpeeled weight
1 tsp lemon juice
225 g/8 oz butter, softened, plus
  extra for greasing
100 g/3½ oz soft light brown sugar
100 g/3½ oz caster sugar
1 egg, beaten
225 g/8 oz self-raising flour
150 g/5½ oz rolled oats
85 g/3 oz raisins

1. Preheat the oven to 180°C/350°F/Gas Mark 4. Grease three large baking sheets. Finely dice the apples and toss in the lemon juice.

2. Put the butter, brown sugar and caster sugar into a bowl and cream until light and fluffy. Gradually beat in the egg. Sift in the flour and add the oats, raisins and apple. Mix until thoroughly combined.

3. Place dessertspoons of the mixture on the prepared baking sheets, spaced well apart.

4. Bake in the preheated oven for 12–15 minutes, or until golden around the edges. Leave the cookies to cool on the baking sheets for 5–10 minutes, or until they are firm enough to transfer to a wire rack to cool completely.

APRICOT, MACADAMIA & WHITE CHOCOLATE CHUNK MUFFINS

MAKES: *12* | **PREP:** *15–20 mins* | **COOK:** *20–25 mins*

INGREDIENTS

280 g/10 oz plain flour
1 tbsp baking powder
115 g/4 oz golden caster sugar
85 g/3 oz ready-to-eat dried apricots, chopped
55 g/2 oz macadamia nuts, chopped
55 g/2 oz white chocolate, chopped
2 eggs, beaten
200 ml/7 fl oz buttermilk
100 ml/3½ fl oz sunflower oil

1. Preheat the oven to 200°C/400°F/Gas Mark 6. Place 12 paper cases in a muffin tin or on a baking sheet.

2. Sift together the flour and baking powder into a bowl and stir in the sugar, apricots, nuts and chocolate.

3. Beat together the eggs, buttermilk and oil, then add to the bowl and stir to mix evenly. Do not over-mix.

4. Spoon the mixture into the muffin cases and bake in the preheated oven for 20–25 minutes until well risen.

5. Serve the muffins warm, preferably on the day of making.

ALL-IN-ONE VANILLA
SPONGE CAKE

SERVES: *8* | **PREP:** *20 mins* | **COOK:** *20–25 mins*

INGREDIENTS

225 g/8 oz plain flour
2 tsp baking powder
225 g/8 oz unsalted butter,
softened, plus extra for greasing
225 g/8 oz caster sugar
4 eggs, beaten
1 tsp vanilla extract

FROSTING

140 g/5 oz unsalted butter
200 g/7 oz icing sugar
1 tsp vanilla extract

1. Preheat the oven to 180°C/350°F/Gas Mark 4. Grease two 20-cm/8-inch sandwich tins and line with baking paper.

2. Sift together the flour and baking powder into a mixing bowl and add the butter, sugar, eggs and vanilla extract. Beat with an electric mixer until just smooth.

3. Spoon the mixture into the prepared tins and level the tops. Bake in the preheated oven for 20–25 minutes until risen, golden brown and firm to the touch.

4. Leave to cool in the tins for 5 minutes, then turn out onto a wire rack and leave to cool completely.

5. To make the frosting, put the butter, sugar and vanilla extract into a bowl and beat until smooth and spreadable. Use half the frosting to sandwich the two cakes together and spread the remaining frosting over the top of the cake.

BEETROOT ROULADE WITH CHOCOLATE FILLING

SERVES: *8–10* | **PREP:** *25–30 mins* | **COOK:** *45–50 mins, plus chilling*

INGREDIENTS
ROULADE
280 g/10 oz beetroot, sliced
sunflower oil, for oiling
175 g/6 oz plain flour, plus
  extra for dusting
2 tbsp cocoa powder
1 tsp bicarbonate of soda
4 eggs
200 g/7 oz golden caster sugar,
  plus extra for dusting
2 tsp vanilla extract
115 ml/3¾ fl oz buttermilk
icing sugar, for dusting

FILLING
70 g/2½ oz white chocolate
160 g/5¾ oz cream cheese
35 g/1¼ oz unsalted butter,
  at room temperature
40 g/1½ oz icing sugar, sifted
½ tsp vanilla extract
finely grated rind of 1 tangerine
70 g/2½ oz dried cherries

1. Place the beetroot in a steamer and steam for 30 minutes, then transfer to a blender and purée until smooth. Transfer to a bowl and set aside until needed.

2. Preheat the oven to 190°C/375°F/Gas Mark 5. Oil a 35 x 25-cm/ 14 x 10-inch Swiss roll tin and line with baking paper. Dust with flour, tipping out any excess. Sift the flour, cocoa powder and bicarbonate of soda twice into a bowl. In a separate bowl, beat the eggs and sugar with a hand-held electric mixer for 6–8 minutes until very thick and creamy. Beat in the beetroot purée and vanilla extract. Gradually beat in the flour mixture, alternating with the buttermilk.

3. Pour the mixture into the prepared tin. Bake in the preheated oven for 10–15 minutes, or until the top springs back when lightly pressed. Lightly dust a sheet of greaseproof paper with golden caster sugar. Turn out the cake onto the prepared paper. Peel off the baking paper, then roll up the cake from the narrow end, with the greaseproof paper inside. Leave to cool.

4. To make the filling, put the chocolate into a heatproof bowl set over a saucepan of gently simmering water and heat until melted. Leave to cool slightly, then mix with the cheese, butter, icing sugar, vanilla extract and tangerine rind.

5. Carefully unroll the cake and remove the paper. Spread the filling evenly over the surface. Sprinkle with the cherries, roll up, wrap tightly in clingfilm and chill in the refrigerator for at least 1 hour. Place the roulade on a platter, seam-side down. Remove a thin slice from either end to neaten, then dust with icing sugar, cut into slices and serve.

HOME-MADE JAFFA CAKES

MAKES: *12* | **PREP:** *45 mins, plus chilling, cooling & setting* | **COOK:** *15–20 mins*

INGREDIENTS

70 g/2½ oz orange jelly (6 cubes),
finely chopped
100 ml/3½ fl oz boiling water
100 ml/3½ fl oz orange juice
2 eggs
50 g/1¾ oz caster sugar
50 g/1¾ oz plain flour
15 g/½ oz butter, melted and
cooled, plus extra for greasing
150 g/5½ oz plain chocolate,
broken into pieces

1. Put the jelly and boiling water into a heatproof bowl and stir until the jelly has dissolved. Stir in the orange juice. Line a shallow 20-cm/8-inch square cake tin with clingfilm and pour in the jelly. Chill in the refrigerator for 2 hours until set. Preheat the oven to 180°C/350°F/Gas Mark 4. Grease a 12-hole bun tin.

2. Place the eggs and sugar in a large heatproof bowl set over a saucepan of gently simmering water. Using a hand-held electric mixer, beat together until the mixture is thick and pale and leaves a trail on the surface when the whisk is lifted. Sift in the flour and fold in gently, then pour over the melted butter and fold in.

3. Spoon the mixture into the holes in the prepared tin. Bake in the preheated oven for 10–12 minutes, or until risen and golden. Leave to cool slightly, then loosen the cakes from the tin with a palette knife and transfer to a wire rack to cool.

4. Put the chocolate into a heatproof bowl set over a saucepan of gently simmering water and heat until melted. Leave to cool slightly. Using a 4.5-cm/1¾-inch round cutter, stamp out 12 rounds of jelly. Place a round on each cake. Spoon the melted chocolate over and gently spread to cover the jelly and cake. Leave to set.

MOLTEN MARSHMALLOW
CHOCOLATE CHUNK BROWNIES

MAKES: *12* | **PREP:** *20 mins* | **COOK:** *50–55 mins*

INGREDIENTS

250 g/9 oz unsalted butter, plus
  extra for greasing
250 g/9 oz plain chocolate
4 large eggs
350 g/12 oz caster sugar
½ tsp vanilla extract
½ tsp salt
150 g/5½ oz plain flour
75 g/2¾ oz large chocolate buttons
  or chocolate chunks
75 g/2¾ oz marshmallow fluff

1. Preheat the oven to 180°C/350°F/Gas Mark 4. Grease a 22-cm/
8½-inch square baking tin and line with baking paper.

2. Put the butter and chocolate into a heatproof bowl set over a
saucepan of gently simmering water and heat, stirring occasionally,
until melted. Remove from the heat and leave to cool slightly. Beat
together the eggs, sugar, vanilla extract and salt in a bowl or jug.

3. Beat the egg mixture into the cooled chocolate mixture, then fold
in the flour. Stir in half the chocolate buttons, pour into the prepared
tin and bake in the preheated oven for 30 minutes.

4. Carefully remove the brownie from the oven (do not switch off the
oven) and add spoonfuls of the marshmallow fluff to the top.

5. Scatter with the remaining chocolate buttons and bake for
a further 10–15 minutes until the marshmallow is molten and
beginning to colour. Leave to cool slightly, then cut into 12 squares
and serve.

CARROT, FRUIT
& CARDAMOM BUNS

MAKES: *16* | **PREP:** *25–30 mins, plus standing* | **COOK:** *30–45 mins*

INGREDIENTS

140 g/5 oz carrots

375 g/13 oz strong white flour,
   sifted, plus extra for dusting

2 tbsp easy-blend dried yeast

3 tbsp golden caster sugar

2 tsp ground cardamom seeds
   (from about 24 pods)

½ tsp salt

125 g/4½ oz unsalted butter

1 egg, lightly beaten

5 tbsp lukewarm milk

sunflower oil, for oiling

150 g/5½ oz chopped glacé fruit

1 egg yolk

1 tbsp cold milk

icing sugar, for dusting

1. Place the carrots in a steamer and steam for 15 minutes until tender, then purée in a blender until smooth. Set aside until needed.

2. Line a baking tray with a silicone sheet. Put the flour, yeast, caster sugar, cardamom and salt into a large bowl and mix to combine. Melt all but 2 tablespoons of the butter and leave to cool slightly. Mix the egg with the milk and the melted butter. Stir into the flour mixture, then add the carrot purée and mix to a soft dough.

3. Turn out the dough onto a work surface lightly dusted with flour and knead for 10–15 minutes until silky. Transfer to a lightly oiled bowl, cover with clingfilm and leave to stand in a warm place for 1½–2 hours, or until doubled in size. Turn out onto a floured surface and knock back. Very thinly roll out to a 44 x 30-cm/ 17½ x 12-inch rectangle.

4. Melt the remaining butter and brush it over the surface of the dough. Scatter over the glacé fruit, taking it right to the edge of the dough and breaking up any clumps.

5. Roll up the dough from the long edge into a log. Slice into 2.5-cm/1-inch rounds and place on the prepared baking tray. Cover with clingfilm and leave to stand for 30 minutes. Meanwhile, preheat the oven to 200°C/400°F/Gas Mark 6.

6. Mix the egg yolk with the cold milk and brush over the buns, then bake in the preheated oven for 10–15 minutes until golden. Transfer to a wire rack to cool, then dust with icing sugar. The buns are best eaten freshly baked.

COURGETTE & WALNUT ROLLS

MAKES: *8* | **PREP:** *25 mins, plus rising* | **COOK:** *10–12 mins*

INGREDIENTS

*450 g/1 lb mixed grain wholemeal
   flour, plus extra for dusting*

1 tsp caraway seeds

1 tsp sea salt

2 tbsp dark molasses sugar

25 g/1 oz butter

2 tsp easy-blend dried yeast

*200 g/7 oz courgettes, coarsely
   grated*

150 ml/5 fl oz lukewarm water

*55 g/2 oz walnut pieces, roughly
   chopped*

1 tbsp olive oil, for oiling

1. Line two baking sheets with non-stick baking paper.

2. Put the flour, caraway seeds, salt, sugar and butter into a mixing bowl and rub in the butter until the mixture resembles fine crumbs. Stir in the yeast.

3. Mix in the courgettes, then add the warm water and mix to a soft dough. Turn out the dough onto a work surface lightly dusted with flour, add the walnuts and knead for 5 minutes until the dough is smooth and elastic.

4. Cut the dough into eight pieces, then place on the prepared baking sheets. Loosely cover the tops with a piece of oiled clingfilm and leave to rise in a warm place for 45 minutes–1 hour.

5. Meanwhile, preheat the oven to 220°C/425°F/Gas Mark 7. Remove the clingfilm, dust the tops of the rolls with a little flour and bake in the preheated oven for 10–12 minutes until golden brown and the bread sounds hollow when tapped on the base. Turn out onto a wire rack and leave to cool completely. Store any leftover rolls in an airtight container and eat within 2–3 days.

CHEESE & HERB SCONES

MAKES: 16 | **PREP:** 20–25 mins | **COOK:** 15–20 mins

INGREDIENTS

5 sprays cooking spray, for oiling

335 g/11¾ oz self-raising wholemeal flour

335 g/11¾ oz white self-raising flour, plus extra for dusting

½ tsp baking powder

¼ tsp salt

75 g/2¾ oz baking margarine (from a block), chopped

100 g/3½ oz mature Cheddar cheese, shredded

1½ tbsp finely snipped fresh chives

1 tbsp finely chopped fresh rosemary leaves

300 ml/10 fl oz milk, plus extra if needed

25 g/1 oz freshly grated Parmesan cheese

1. Preheat the oven to 220°C/425°F/Gas Mark 7. Spray a large baking tray with cooking spray.

2. Sift the wholemeal flour, white flour, baking powder and salt into a mixing bowl, tipping in any bran left in the sieve, and stir to combine. Add the margarine and rub it into the flour with your fingertips until the mixture resembles breadcrumbs. Stir in the Cheddar cheese, chives and rosemary.

3. Make a well in the centre of the dry ingredients and pour in all but 2 tablespoons of the milk, stirring with a metal spatula until a dough begins to form, then finish the process using your hands. If necessary, add a little more milk or water (you need only enough to form a stiff dough).

4. Turn out onto a work surface lightly dusted with flour and gently knead to a smooth dough. Add more flour to the work surface and the rolling pin if necessary, then roll out the dough to a thickness of 2 cm/¾ inch. Cut out 16 scones with a 7.5-cm/3-inch round cutter.

5. Put the scones on the prepared tray, evenly spaced out. Brush the tops with the remaining milk, then sprinkle over the Parmesan cheese. Bake in the preheated oven for 15–20 minutes, or until the scones are golden and cooked through, and sound hollow when tapped on the base. Serve warm or cold. The scones can be frozen for up to 1 month.

PUMPKIN &
PEPITA MUFFINS

MAKES: *12* | **PREP:** *25–30 mins* | **COOK:** *30 mins*

INGREDIENTS

light olive oil, for oiling
250 g/9 oz peeled, deseeded
  pumpkin, cut into 1-cm/½-inch
  dice
4-cm/1½-inch piece fresh ginger,
  scrubbed and roughly grated
3 eggs
4 tbsp maple syrup
225 g/8 oz natural yogurt
150 g/5½ oz wholemeal flour
100 g/3½ oz fine cornmeal
3 tsp baking powder
1 tsp mixed spice
3 tbsp pepita (pumpkin) seeds

1. Preheat the oven to 190°C/375°F/Gas Mark 5. Lightly brush a 12-hole muffin tin with oil.

2. Place the pumpkin in the top of a steamer set over a saucepan of gently simmering water, cover and cook for 15 minutes until just soft. Mash well, add the ginger and mix to combine.

3. Place the eggs, maple syrup and yogurt in a medium-sized bowl and whisk together.

4. Put the flour, cornmeal, baking powder and mixed spice into a large bowl and stir together, then add the mashed pumpkin and egg mixture and briefly whisk together until just combined.

5. Spoon the batter into the prepared tin, sprinkle with the pepita seeds, then bake in the preheated oven for 15 minutes until well risen and golden brown. Leave to cool in the tin for 5 minutes, then loosen the edges with a knife, turn out onto a wire rack and leave to cool completely. These are best eaten within 2 days of making.

PUMPERNICKEL BREAD

MAKES: *1 loaf* | **PREP:** *25–30 mins, plus rising* | **COOK:** *1 hour*

INGREDIENTS

75 g/2¾ oz quick-cook polenta

300 ml/10 fl oz cold water

60 g/2¼ oz molasses sugar

1 tbsp light olive oil

1½ tsp salt

2 tsp caraway seeds

1 tbsp cocoa powder

225 g/8 oz cold or lukewarm mashed potatoes

400 g/14 oz dark rye flour

150 g/5½ oz plain wholemeal flour, plus extra for dusting

15 g/½ oz easy-blend dried yeast

100 ml/3½ fl oz lukewarm water

5 sprays cooking spray, for oiling

1. Put the polenta into a saucepan with the cold water and cook over a low heat, stirring constantly, for 5 minutes, or until it has thickened to a porridge-like consistency. Remove from the heat and add the sugar, oil, salt, caraway seeds and cocoa powder. Stir to combine and leave to cool slightly.

2. Stir in the mashed potatoes, then add the rye flour, wholemeal flour, yeast and lukewarm water and knead for 10 minutes, or until the dough is smooth and pliable.

3. Spray a large bowl with cooking spray and place the dough in the bowl. Cover with a clean tea towel and leave to stand in a warm place for around 45 minutes, or until doubled in size.

4. Meanwhile, preheat the oven to 190°C/375°F/Gas Mark 5. Spray a 1-kg/2 lb 4-oz loaf tin with cooking spray.

5. Put the dough into the prepared tin, shaping it to fit. Make a few diagonal cuts along the top and sprinkle with a little wholemeal flour. Bake in the preheated oven for 1 hour, or until the loaf sounds hollow when tapped on the base. Leave to cool in the tin for 10 minutes, then transfer to a wire rack and leave to cool completely.

This edition published by Parragon Books Ltd in 2017
LOVE FOOD is an imprint of Parragon Books Ltd

Parragon Books Ltd
Chartist House
15–17 Trim Street
Bath BA1 1HA, UK
www.parragon.co.uk/love-food
www.parragon.com.au/love-food

ISBN 978-1-4748-6896-9

Printed in China

Introduction by Sarah Bush
Edited by Fiona Biggs
Cover photography by Al Richardson

The cover shot shows the Chilli con Carne on page 151.

.... *Notes for the Reader* ....

This book uses both metric and imperial measurements.
Follow the same units of measurement throughout;
do not mix metric and imperial. All spoon measurements
are level: teaspoons are assumed to be 5 ml, and tablespoons
are assumed to be 15 ml. Unless otherwise stated, milk
is assumed to be full fat, eggs and individual fruits and
vegetables are medium, pepper is freshly ground black
pepper and salt is table salt. Unless otherwise stated,
all root vegetables should be peeled prior to using.

The times given are an approximate guide only.
Preparation times differ according to the techniques used
by different people and the cooking times may also vary
from those given.